The Theatrical Vocal Music
of
Nancy Van de Vate

Volume I 1958-2000

by

Michelle Vought

Interior Graphics/Art Credit: Nancy Van de Vate

ISBN: 978-1-4834-2044-8 (sc)
ISBN: 978-1-4834-2043-1 (e)

Lulu Publishing Services rev. date: 12/12/2014

CONTENTS

PREFACE

Twentieth-century theater music provides an ideal vehicle with which composers, performers, and listeners can explore and become familiar with contemporary idioms. Audiences find theater pieces accessible because of the dramatic features of staging, lighting, properties, costumes, and characterization; listeners seem more open to musical innovation in such a context. Composers, while using the tools of a broad twentieth-century musical language, can create through this amalgamation of music and theater a unique product of self-expression.

As a performer, I have a special interest in twentieth-century music, particularly theater music, and find it not only very engaging, but also challenging and extremely gratifying to perform. I know that my ear, as well as my overall musicianship, continues to improve with each new piece. Of the four works discussed here, I have performed in three, and each performance was a unique experience, both for me and for the audience

This project was first undertaken as my dissertation for the Doctor of Musical Arts degree in Vocal Performance at the Cincinnati College-Conservatory of Music. It is fortunate that since that time all of the works discussed have been professionally recorded and released on compact disc, making my commentary more immediately accessible. These recordings are now also universally available over the Internet from Naxos Music Library or on You Tube

I am deeply indebted to Nancy Van de Vate and her colleague Meaghan Burke for their assistance in preparing the material for publication and hope this book not only illustrates the excellence of the four works included, but also brings a broader understanding to all contemporary theatrical vocal music.

Michelle Vought
Normal, Illinois, June 2014

CHAPTER ONE

Biography

Nancy Van de Vate, born Nancy Jean Hayes on December 30, 1930, in Plainfield, New Jersey, studied piano as a young girl and made her debut as a concert pianist in 1946. During her high school years, her piano teacher, Mary Grissom of Plainfield, recognizing her unusual talent, arranged a scholarship for additional study with master teacher, Anton Rovinsky, who came to Plainfield once each week from New York. Van de Vate worked with Mr. Rovinsky for one year, then in 1948 entered the Eastman School of Music in Rochester, NY, as a piano performance major, studying with Cécile Genhart.

After one year of intensive study at Eastman, Van de Vate transferred as a sophomore to Wellesley College in Massachusetts. Wanting a somewhat broader education leading to both the Bachelor of Music and Bachelor of Arts degrees, her plan was to return to Eastman every summer, then for an additional year, to complete a B.Mus. in piano, having already completed a B.A. in music theory at Wellesley.

In the summer of 1950, after her first year at Wellesley, she returned to Eastman, again studying piano with Cécile Genhart.

The following summer, however, she spent in Europe, working at a children's camp in Menton, France for several weeks, then traveling in Italy and England. On June 9, 1952 she married Dwight Van de Vate, Jr. in the Wellesley College Chapel after having graduated earlier that day. The couple moved to New Haven, Connecticut, where they remained until the summer of 1955, and Van de Vate did not return to Eastman to complete the Bachelor of Music degree.

However, in 1954 she resumed studying piano with Bruce Simonds of the Yale School of Music. After her husband accepted his first teaching position at the University of Mississippi in the fall of 1955, she began to study music composition there with Arthur Kreutz. In 1958 she became the first person to be awarded the Master of Music degree in composition by that institution. In 1963 Van de Vate entered the doctoral program in composition at Florida State University, studying with John Boda. She completed the D. Mus. in 1968, the first woman to earn that degree in composition at Florida State, which awarded no further doctorates in composition to women until the late 1970s. She later undertook post-doctoral study in electronic music as a participant in the 1972 Summer Electronic Music Institute at Dartmouth College and the University of New Hampshire.

Throughout her career, Van de Vate has worked as a private piano teacher, music critic, lecturer, and composer-in-residence, as well as instructor, assistant, associate, and full professor of music and academic dean at many American colleges and universities. She has taught in a variety of musical areas, including theory, history, analysis, composition, piano, and choral arranging. She has always been actively involved in professional musical organizations: the Southeastern Composers League, of which she was president from 1973-75, Broadcast Music, Inc., the American Composers Alliance, the National Academy of Recording Arts and Sciences, the Music Critics

Association, the International Society for Contemporary Music, and more recently, various European composers' organizations.

Early in her career, Van de Vate recognized the need for an organization which would provide greater professional opportunities for women composers. With that vision, she founded the League of Women Composers in 1975. Though this organization began in the United States, it soon expanded to other countries, and subsequently it became the International League of Women Composers. In 1990 she co-founded with her late husband, Clyde Smith, the nonprofit classical music recording company, Vienna Modern Masters. Specializing in new music for large orchestra, the VMM catalog now includes 145 compact discs.

The composer's dedication, talent, and hard work have been rewarded by international recognition and critical acclaim. In 1975 she received the first place award for Quintet for Brass in the Delius Composition Contest; in 1979, first prize for Quintet 1975 in the Los Alamos Chamber Music Competition. 1987 brought a Composer's Fellowship from the United States National Endowment for the Arts for *Chernobyl*, 1988 a Maryland State Arts Council Composer's Fellowship, and 1989 a Work-in-Progress Award for *Katyn*. She has also received numerous grants from the Austrian government. Her articles have appeared in many periodicals including *Musical America, Symphony News, The Music Educators Journal, The Instrumentalist*, and *International Musician*.

The eclecticism of Van de Vate's distinctive style is largely the result of her extensive travels; she has lived throughout the continental United States and in Hawaii, as well as in Indonesia and Vienna. Her music is regularly presented at festivals in Munich, Vienna, Salzburg, Heidelberg, Bremen, Poznan, and many other locations. Known primarily for music in the large forms, she has composed twenty-six orchestral works and ten operas and music theater pieces. *All Quiet on the Western Front*, based on the novel by Remarque, was completed in 1999; *Hamlet*, based on Shakespeare's drama, was completed in 2009; and *Where the Cross Is Made*, a chamber opera based on the play by Eugene O'Neill, was finished in 2003.

Van de Vate is not only the most recorded American woman composer of orchestral music now on compact disc, she is also thought to be the most recorded woman composer of classical music in the world. Her orchestral works have been released on the Conifer (UK), Leonarda, Live from the Louisiana Sinfonietta and Vienna Modern Masters labels and have received numerous Pulitzer Prize and Grawemeyer Award nominations. She has been recognized with commissions and awards from the American Association of University Women's Education and Research Fund, Meet the Composer, and the Money for Women/Barbara Deming Memorial Fund. She was a Resident Fellow at Yaddo, the MacDowell Colony, and Ossabaw Island in the United States, and at the Tyrone Guthrie Center at Annaghmakerrig (Ireland), the Brahmshaus (Baden-Baden, Germany), and the Künstlerhaus Boswil (Switzerland).

Van de Vate who now resides in Vienna, holds dual Austrian and American citizenship and gives frequent lectures about her music in both English and German in Europe, Asia, and North America. Her music has been heard in at least 40 countries on five continents.

Style

Perhaps Van de Vate's success as a composer can be attributed to her pragmatic and unpretentious approach. Well aware that composition is hard work, she treats each piece as a tool for honing her compositional craft. Always willing to make necessary compromises when musical conditions warrant it, she believes firmly that "to improve as a composer, everything must be performed, even if not well."[1] Because of this strong commitment to live performance, she seeks every possible opportunity to hear her music and utilizes all available resources.

Also firmly committed to the exploration of new sounds and media, Van de Vate has experimented with many techniques and styles of composition. However, her favorite genre (and greatest strength) lies in composing large-scale works with orchestra. In recent years, she has combined this passion for orchestral writing with her early interest in operatic composition. Opera has proven to be quite a natural medium for her, as it brings together her immense skill in orchestration, her dramatic flair, love of literature, and deftness in setting texts.

Van de Vate's eclectic style has been shaped by a wide range of influences. She herself credits Bela Bartok, Igor Stravinsky, Krzysztof Penderecki, and Edgar Varèse for having the most profound effect on her compositional choices. Admiration for the timbral features of Bartok's music, particularly in *Music for Strings, Percussion, and Celesta*, and for the linear aspects of his counterpoint inspired the imaginative interplay between color and line found in many of her works. The imagistic quality of Stravinsky's early, pre-twelve-tone works is also reflected in Van de Vate's music. The brutal directness and relentless rhythmic drive of such works as *The Firebird* and *The Rite of Spring* (which she regards as perhaps the greatest work of the twentieth century), as well as their highly dramatic aspects, infuse many of her compositions.

---

[1]   Nancy Van de Vate, interview with Michelle Vought, August 1, 1993, tape recording, Vienna, Austria.

Van de Vate admires the direct emotional impact and tone color experimentation of Krzysztof Penderecki, while her concept of sound mass reveals the influence of Varèse, its inventor and one of the first composers to place primary emphasis on sonority. Her fondness for unconventional tone colors was particularly gratified during her time in Indonesia, where she lived for almost four years. There she became acquainted with the zither-like *kecapi* and especially the gamelan, whose sounds and textures she has incorporated into many of her compositions.

In discussing how she composes, Van de Vate admits to writing very little at the piano. With the advantage of absolute pitch, she first forms ideas in her head, outlining materials within a skeleton of precise rhythms, then transferring these quickly to the manuscript. She considers timbre to be her primary organizational and structural element, sometimes building pieces largely out of sound masses, from which melodies emerge. In a *Pan Pipes* article, Jocelyn Mackey comments,

> Van de Vate's interest in orchestral colors is evident,
> as is her skill and imagination in selecting and using
> them. An important aspect of her attitude seems to be
> that she obtains wonderful effects within the expected
> parameters of instruments without seeming to strain
> them beyond their limits.[2]

Eschewing the notion of being an "innovator," Van de Vate rarely incorporates unconventional uses of instruments, though she

---

[2]   Jocelyn Mackey, "Review of Nancy Van de Vate, Distant Worlds, Dark Nebulae, Journeys, Concertpiece for Cello and Small Orchestra," Pan Pipes # 2, (Winter 1988); p. 15.

occasionally uses extended piano techniques--for example, requiring the performer to pluck piano strings or strike them with rubber mallets. In her vocal piece, Cocaine Lil, she somewhat uncharacteristically unleashes a whole arsenal of extended vocal techniques, including tongue rolls, ascending and descending tongue flutters, and tongue clicks. This particular segment, sung almost entirely on vowel sounds, serves as a cadenza (see Example 1). It is interesting to note, however, that the work's melodic and rhythmic precision suggest an instrumentally conceived piece. Example 1 also illustrates Van de Vate's consistent use of conventional notation.

Example 1.

Shimmering tone colors reflect the influence of Indonesian music, while her somber, dark timbres draw more on the character of Polish music, according to Kyle Gann. He calls her sound a "dark, timbre-oriented, sound-mass-filled idiom characteristic of the Polish school."[3] *Distant Worlds*, for solo violin and orchestra, offers a fine example: a dense, layered texture of chord colors in blocks is penetrated by individual melodies, which weave plaintively in and out of the sound mass.

Van de Vate's sound has been described as both cleansing and bracing. Kurt Loft praises her directness, stating that "the music stabs directly at its subject and shocks it to life."[4]

Referring to Penderecki and Van de Vate, Loft continues:

> They do not write happy tunes, but harrowing compositions that sear rather than please the ear, just as the late string quartets of Beethoven confused a generation of 19th-century listeners...somber and dark, many of their works reflect the anguish and arrogance of mankind.[5]

These blocks of sound with interwoven melodies are not static but include distinct points of arrival and departure, since Van de Vate believes strongly that a piece should have narrative direction. An efficient composer and frequent reviser, she eliminates extraneous elements, maintaining precision and succinctness above all else. She avoids extensive divisi, writes almost exclusively in meters, and includes very little aleatory. What aleatory she does use is typically for percussion, as in the middle section of *Distant Worlds*.

---

[3]   Kyle Gann, "Review of Nancy Van de Vate, Distant Worlds, Dark Nebulae, Journeys, Concertpiece for Cello and Small Orchestra," Fanfare 11, #3 (January, February, 1988), p. 224.

[4]   Kurt Loft, "Tones of Anguish," The Tampa Tribune, May 21, 1989.

[5]   *ibid*

Van de Vate claims that her music, with its deeply atmospheric and evocative qualities, is not overtly programmatic. Her goal is to evoke feelings, not to recount a story. Believing that music should "speak directly to the listener,"[6] she sometimes employs musical quotations for their powerful associations. In her *Krakow Concerto*, for instance, she borrows the trumpet signal played hourly from the tower of St. Mary's church in the Krakow market square. Other examples include a Russian folk tune in *Chernobyl*, a Polish folk song and the Dies Irae in *Katyn*, an excerpt from Stravinsky's L'Histoire du Soldat in her Concerto for Violin and Orchestra, and Chopin's "Marche funèbre" from his Piano Sonata in B-flat minor in *Cocaine Lil* (see Examples 2 and 3).

Example 2. Chopin, Frederic, *Piano Sonata, B flat Minor, Opus 35, Third Movement*

---

[6]   Nancy Van de Vate, interview by Michelle Vought, August 1, 1993, tape recording, Vienna, Austria.

Example 3. *Cocaine Lil*, p. 18

Another of Van de Vate's preferred emotive devices is the tone cluster. Stephen Ellis notes that "at the end of *Katyn* even the voices have succumbed to Penderecki-like clustering – heard naturally as the inevitable anguish of souls in torment."[7] Van de Vate also frequently uses *ostinati* to build tension in her works.

Though her music is primarily atonal, it is always lyrical and rarely harsh harmonically. The composer admits to having a subconscious

7   Stephen Ellis, "Review of Nancy Van de Vate, Krakow Concerto for percussion and orchestra, Katyn for orchestra and chorus," Fanfare 14, #4 (March/April 1991): p. 411.

penchant for the Phrygian mode, with its minor second between the first two steps of the scale; she often employs this mode for its sad, mournful sound, as heard in her Nine Preludes for Piano.

Perhaps Van de Vate's most unusual and interesting innovation is a compositional device she calls "smudging," which she defines as "the use of quiet rapid background figures, sometimes random and sometimes precise, played simultaneously with more sharply etched melodic lines."[8] *Dark Nebulae*, composed in Honolulu in 1981, exemplifies this technique (see Example 4).

---

[8]   Kurt Loft, "Tones of Anguish," The Tampa Tribune, May 21, 1989.

Example 4. *Dark Nebulae*, mm. 60-63.

Van de Vate divides her music, which she maintains represents no special school or ideology, into four stylistic periods. She comments however, that some elements of her style, such as scale patterns and methods of contrasting dynamics and tempi, are omnipresent. Her first stylistic period, during which she lived in Mississippi, dates from 1955 to 1963. Employing mostly traditional triadic harmonies, she began experimenting with quartal harmonies under lyrical, sometimes modal melodies. Her style was somewhat contrapuntal, touching on pandiatonicism. A typical piece from this "Mississippi Period" is the song "Youthful Age" (1960) for voice and piano. (see Example 5).

Example 5. *Youthful Age,* mm. 4-7.

Note the reinforcement of the vocal melody in the piano's top line, which is supported by quartal harmonies.

Van de Vate's "American Period" spans the next eight years, 1964-1972. Her music from this period, straying from diatonicism into chromaticism, displays the pronounced influence of Bartok. The song *To the East and to the West* (1972) is a characteristic example of her vocal style during this time (see Example 6), while her sonatas exemplify her use of Bartokian "random, dissonant counterpoint."[9]

Examples 6. *To the East and to the West*, mm. 23-30.

From ca. 1972-81, Van de Vate engaged in what she terms her period of "exploration and discovery,"[10] during which she found new paths of expression and methods of composition. The 1972 Institute on Electronic Music sparked Van de Vate's now defining interest in timbre. As she endowed color with greater importance, she began to perceive color itself as a potential point of origin for a composition. Placing less emphasis on line and form and more emphasis on overall sound, she started to use clusters for the first time. She was careful to maintain order and structure, however, and almost invariably rounded off pieces by returning to the opening material at the end.

---

[9]   Nancy Van de Vate, interview by Michelle Vought, August 1, 1993, tape recording, Vienna, Austria.

[10]   *ibid*

A Night in the Royal Ontario Museum dates from 1983, but it could certainly be considered a product of Van de Vate's "exploratory" period. Scored for soprano and tape, it includes many unconventional sounds, both acoustic and electronic, and provides an excellent example of her fondness for timbral experimentation. Drawing on minimal resources, the composer produces a thoroughly engaging and unusual masterpiece for the concert hall. *A Night in the Royal Ontario Museum* will be the first work discussed in this study of her theatrical vocal music.

CHAPTER TWO

A Night in the Royal Ontario Museum

Profile of the Work

Van de Vate composed the atonal dramatic scena for soprano and tape, *A Night in the Royal Ontario Museum*, (1983) at the request of a soprano friend, Marilyn Boyd de Reggi. Using a poem by Canadian author Margaret Atwood, Van de Vate created a twelve-minute piece with minimal staging and lighting and maximal dramatic effect. Slides picturing artifacts from the Royal Ontario Museum are available and may also be used in performance. The text, written in first person, describes the character's experience as she wanders through the dimly lit museum in which she was accidentally locked overnight. For discussion purposes, I have divided the poem into seven sections.

PART A: SETTING THE SCENE

Who locked me into this crazed man/made
brain, stone-brain
Where the weather'd totem pole jabs a
blunt finger

At the Byzantine mosaic dome
Under that ornate golden cranium
I wander among the fragments of gods,
tarnished coins, embalmed gestures
chronologically arranged,
Looking for the EXIT sign
But in spite of the diagrams at every
corner, labelled in red: YOU ARE
HERE
The labyrinth holds me

PART B: DESCRIBING THE ACTIVITY

Turning me around, around, around,
turning me around,
Around, around the cafeteria, the
washrooms, a spiral through
Greece and Rome,
The bronze horses of China
Then past the carved masks, wood and fur
to where five plaster Indians in a
glass case squat near a dusty fire
And further confronting me with a skeleton
child, child
Preserved, preserved, preserved in the
desert air,
And further confronting me, confronting
me, confronting me, confronting me
With a skeleton child, curled, curled,
beside a clay pot and a few beads

18

PART C: PLEADING WITH THE MUSEUM

I say I am far enough, stop here please,

I say I am far enough, stop here

Please no more

But the perverse museum corridor by

corridor repeats, repeats,

Repeats its memories,

PART D: SPONTANEOUS REACTION

An idiot voice jogged by a pushed button

I am dragged to the mind's dead-end,

the roar of the bone-yard,

PART E: RESIGNATION

I am lost among the mastodons and beyond

A fossil shell, samples of rocks and

Minerals

Even the thundering tusks dwindling to

pinpoints in the stellar fluorescent

lighted wastes of geology.

PART F: REVEALING DESPAIR

I say I am far enough, stop here please,

I say I am far enough, no more

PART G: SURRENDER

But the perverse museum corridor by corridor
Repeats its memories, memories
Repeats, repeats, repeats its memories,
Memories, memories.

Each section of the poem has its own purpose in the dramatic scheme of the work, a sort of psychological destination. Operatic in nature, the work at times reveals a conventional recitative/aria-like design in which the soprano narrates the activity in which she is engaged, then reflects emotionally on what has occurred. In the beginning, the text describes the museum's physical structure and its exhibits. As it continues, the soprano becomes increasingly agitated and emotional, vacillating ever more frequently between calm and hysteria. The text's division into many short sections in the latter half of the poem reflects the character's deteriorating mental state.

Van de Vate's music heightens the drama of the character's psychological journey, endowing the museum with a persona of its own. The conflict between the soprano and the museum deepens over the course of the poem until the soprano actually submits herself to her nemesis at the scene's conclusion. A detailed account of Van de Vate's musical setting will be presented later in the chapter.

At first, the character in the poem describes in rather straightforward, rational terms what she is seeing, doing, and feeling. As her anxiety increases, however, she confronts the museum more and more as though it were a person, pleading: "I say I am far enough, stop here please, please no more" (Sections C and F). Van de Vate makes the most of these sections, enabling the audience to witness the singer's emotional roller coaster. In so doing, she integrates the Atwood character's stream of consciousness with her own interpretation of the character's disintegrating psyche.

The tape component of the work employs almost exclusively *musique concrète*. To create the tape portion, Van de Vate layered acoustically produced sounds by copying them back and forth on two open-reel tape recorders. By changing the speed of the tape, she was able to alter pitch and register to create a wide array of tone colors. Attempting to use the simplest resources, Van de Vate produced sounds with basic household items such as pots and pans, as well as employing microphone feedback to create a howling sound. She also incorporates the sounds of the *kecapi* (the zither-like Indonesian instrument mentioned in the previous chapter) and a small hand-held drum from Sumatra, thus revealing the influence of Jakarta, Indonesia, where she composed this piece. Throughout the work, one can also detect the somewhat more familiar sounds of slide whistles and piano strings being plucked and strummed.

Simply by examining the first page of the score, one can make some general observations about the nature of the work (see Example 7).

Example 7. *A Night in the Royal Ontario Museum*, p.1.

© 1983 by Nancy Van de Vate

First of all, Van de Vate uses conventional notation, with one system for the tape and one for the soprano. Her notation of the tape part is somewhat pictorial in its reflection of what sounds the tape offers, e.g. slanting lines for glissandi and sidewise black triangle for a decaying boom. She avoids using bar lines to mark measures, but instead uses an occasional vertical dotted line to indicate places where the tape and voice need to be aligned. Though the piece is unmetered, very clear durational values appear. The tempo ♩=50 will change abruptly and frequently (most often to ♩=63, also sometimes by means of *accelerandi* and *ritardandi*. Dynamics shift as frequently as tempi, with sudden and rapid changes and hairpins on a single quarter note, or even an eighth note.

Instructions for articulation and expression are also frequent and specific, Within seconds of the soprano's entrance Van de Vate indicates how two consecutive passages should be sung: the first, "man-made brain," uses an accent on "brain," then a downward *portamento;* the second, "stone brain," requires accents on each word, sung with no vibrato and with no connection between them. Midway through the score, Van de Vate indicates that the text should be "spoken wearily," following an *ad libitum* section which is marked "rapidly, hysterically, with an angular jagged line." She also gives highly precise timings indicating when textual/musical events should occur.

Atwood's text is set syllabically, with some spoken portions, in highly disjunct lines. Van de Vate often employs the minor second and tritone intervals, but larger intervals, such as the major seventh, as well as wide leaps of almost two octaves, occur later in the work. She incorporates a wide variety of vocal techniques, including trills, glissandi, touches of *Sprechstimme*, straight tone, and a short section of directed aleatory.

When looking at the score and listening to the tape part alone, it sounds as though the singer and tape will be in dialogue. Their relationship, however, can be viewed from several perspectives. The tape is, at various points throughout the *scena*, a character in and of itself, an accompaniment to the soprano's character, and a representation of her subconscious. At times, the tape recedes, allowing the soprano to dominate, while at other times the tape interrupts the singer to achieve aural dominance. The progression of the tape's musical function parallels the psychological course of the soprano's erratic behavior, with high points of sound and drama followed by dramatic silences.

The recorded sound and the voice become increasingly integrated as the shift in the soprano's psyche leads to less "human" sounds: harsh articulations, extreme range demands, abrupt dynamic shifts, pointillistic melodies, and extended vocal techniques. This process ultimately brings about a complete fusion of the two, as both soprano and tape sing a unison high E for eight full beats.

Throughout the piece are precisely timed tape interpolations, labeled "sound collages," from which the voice takes its cue. Although these collages are carefully composed, they create a sense of utter chaos, with no apparent rhythmic, melodic, or formal structure. This apparent randomness, coupled with Van de Vate's extensive experimentation with timbre, creates an effect of pandemonium and disorientation. These collages give the tape a personality of its own, one which antagonizes the singer, shocking and taunting her into madness. At the piece's conclusion, slide whistles enter sardonically, setting off the soprano's final bout of hysteria. The performer should react to the multitude of evocative sound effects throughout the piece, including a taunting, echoing voice; high, prickly piano strings (both plucked and strummed); knocks; low, sustained ringing sounds;

drums, and glissandi. The final glissando, like the slide whistles before, adds a tone of mockery and sarcasm.

At the outset of the piece, the tape accompaniment seems to derive from an almost science fiction-like world of chaos and unreality, while the singer comes from one of order and sanity. The performer and audience are drawn into the unfamiliar, unsafe world of the tape, eventually losing contact with reality. As the soprano wanders through the museum, she adopts characteristics resembling those of the tape, eventually losing her bearings, mind, and humanity, and merging with the tape, whose final relentless drone suggests that the battle is finished--in the museum's favor. Its final glissando represents the museum's one last triumphant, mocking laugh as the already dim lights are extinguished and darkness falls.

Musical and Dramatic Flow

The eerie setting of Margaret Atwood's poem "A Night in the Royal Ontario Museum" lends itself well to the electronic medium and its timbral possibilities. Van de Vate capitalizes on this, using a subtle manipulation of text and timbre to create a fascinating psychological drama, one that is gratifying, accessible, and engaging to performer and audience alike.

At the beginning of the piece, the tape is heard alone for over one minute. The soprano may enter the stage at any time during this sparsely textured introduction of glissandi, gongs, and *kecapi*. These spooky sound effects heighten the sense of her aloneness as she sings, "Who locked me…" In Van de Vate's setting, these words take on an accusatory, almost confrontational tone, with the melody leaping up a major seventh and an abrupt dynamic shifts to reveal the soprano's agitation.

Example 8. *A Night in the Royal Ontario Museum*, p. 1.

The soprano's wearied annoyance is depicted musically with heavy accents and straight tone, along with an increase in dynamic level. For the first time since the soprano's entrance, the tape intrudes with a unison half note on the gong and the *kecapi*, punctuating the soprano's initial utterances. When the singer chants, "Under that ornate golden cranium, I wander among…," she admits that she is lost, wandering aimlessly with no strategy for escape. Van de Vate sets the next series of phrases in a haunting ascending and descending ostinato on the pitches C#, D#, and E. This circular pattern, looping aimlessly around one note, reflects the character's disoriented meandering through the museum.

Example 9. Van de Vate, Nancy, *A Night in the Royal Ontario Museum*, p. 2.

Above the staff, Van de Vate has indicated that the passage is to be sung "tinged with monotony, [in a] somewhat breathy voice." Three phrases later, after seven repetitions of the C#-D#-E motive, she is to return to an ordinary voice with a poco accelerando and crescendo to fortissimo as she sings, "looking for the exit sign." This is her first major outpouring of exasperation and frustration, made all the more brutal by the preceding *ostinato*.

This first outburst is followed by seven seconds of loud drum sounds on the tape, which act to antagonize her. Once the drums have dwindled to a soft rumble, she speaks again: "but in spite of the diagram at every corner labelled in red, 'You are here,' the labyrinth holds me." She comments, somewhat objectively, on the irony that signs meant to orient her do nothing to free her from the maze of twisting passages. Throughout this commentary, the drum sounds continue, soft yet relentless, suggesting a lingering horror that defies any attempt to dispel it with logic.

This horror bursts out in full force with the first sound collage, which lasts for 30 seconds. As with the subsequent collages, this onslaught of inhuman sounds brings the soprano to a new level of agitation, both musically and dramatically. The turmoil is evident as she sings, "Then past the carved masks, wood and fur to where five plaster Indians in a glass case squat near a dusty fire." This passage spans a range of almost two octaves within eight beats and marks the onset of the singer's loss of rationality. She continues:

> And further confronting me with a skeleton child,
> child, preserved, preserved, preserved in the desert
> air and further confronting me, confronting me,
> confronting me, confronting me with a skeleton child,
> curled, curled, beside a clay pot and a few beads.

In order to portray the ghastliness of this diorama, Van de Vate repeats the text several times, with a salient instance of text painting in the vocal flutter on "child" (see Example 10). For an entire page, this text is repeated over the tape's expanding and receding boom.

Example 10. *A Night in the Royal Ontario Museum*, p. 4.

A one-minute fifteen-second sound collage ensues, further increasing the soprano's agitation. As she continues her fruitless search for an exit, she takes on a pleading tone: "I say I am far enough, stop here please, please no more," with a subito piano on "please no more." A nine-second collage arouses her antagonism once again, however, and she enters forte with a highly disjunct line employing a minor tenth leap on the text, "but the perverse museum." At the word "repeats" (in the phrase "but the perverse museum repeats"), she executes a vocal flutter on a descending glissando, stated twice on a vowel of her choice (see Example 11). This extended technique presents yet another indication of the character's approaching madness.

Example 11. *A Night in the Royal Ontario Museum,* p. 6.

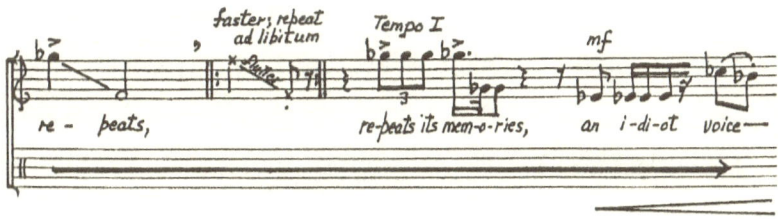

Having triggered a recorded voice at one exhibit by accidentally tapping a button, the soprano refers to "an idiot voice jogged by a pushed button." This phantom voice is heard on the tape, softly speaking words which are unintelligible. (It was created by playing in the reverse direction a tape of the composer speaking in a normal voice). It marks the soprano's final lurch into madness as she exclaims, fortissimo, in a very high register, "I am dragged to the mind's dead-end, the roar of the bone-yard" (see Example 12).

Example 12. *A Night in the Royal Ontario Museum*, p. 7.

Though she could indeed be standing by a exhibit resembling a cemetery, we may assume that she has reached the graveyard of her mental faculties. She is now instructed to "sing rapidly, almost hysterically with an angular, jagged line," fragmenting the *ad libitum* section on the same text. After singing in this manner for 11 seconds, she speaks the text once again, wearily, as if in surrender.

At this point, she seems resigned to her plight and sings slowly and expressively, "I am lost." She strolls through the museum and comments in an ordinary speaking voice on the exhibits before her: "a fossil shell, minerals, samples of rocks." In one final moment of semi-clarity, she begs once more to be released from this misery: "I say I am far enough stop here please, please no more." Her final plea is mocked, however, by the entrance of playful-sounding slide whistles. After executing a few frenzied glissandi, the singer ends this section with a sudden, almost psychotic laugh, as if responding to the whistles (see Example 13); perhaps this cackle is a signal that she has begun to embrace her own madness.

Example 13. *A Night at the Royal Ontario Museum,* p. 9.

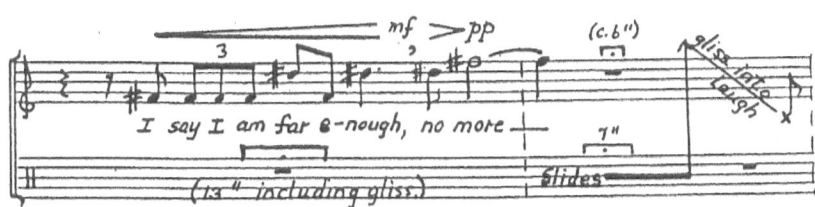

An ominous gong sounds, to which she responds, "but the perverse museum." She is interrupted once again by the jeering of the slide whistles before her final words: "corridor by corridor repeats its memories, repeats its memories, memories, memories." At the close of the piece, the soprano and the museum (as represented by the tape) finish on the same pitch, as if fused together to form one entity. The tape continues after the singer for an eerie 35 seconds of high piano sounds, a gong, and finally, a long ascending tinny glissando. In this final collage, the museum announces its triumph over the prisoner, and proudly displays its newest acquisition.

Performance Considerations

Because of its somewhat static plot, *A Night in the Royal Ontario Museum* is more a character study of a woman's mental deterioration than the unfolding of a story. In preparing the work, the soloist must make some choices regarding characterization and staging. Fortunately, Van de Vate's preface provides staging ideas as well as suggestions about how the piece should progress dramatically.

> The stage should contain a lighted red EXIT sign,
> the suggestion of a display case and a small backless

bench. Lighting should be minimal, primarily a spotlight for the soprano.

The stage should be dark when the piece opens. As the low gong sounds begin, lighting should be brought up gradually and the soprano should emerge from the shadows. During the gong sounds, both high and low, the singer walks around slowly, but distractedly, as if she were trying to find a way out. She pauses here and there as though in front of display cases. Her opening solo is conversational but also tinged with sardonic humor, annoyance and some disgust with the situation. The material on page 3 suggests greater annoyance but not yet real agitation. The singer may wish to sit down during the 30" collage, perhaps with an air of dejection. She will probably wish to stand again during other material on pages 4 and 5, sitting again for the 1'15" collage. Her mood vacillates between annoyance, colored by anxiety, and resignation.

On page 6, third system, the singer begins to feel very agitated, and her anxiety and annoyance climax on page 7. The mood here may verge on hysteria. Resignation takes over again on pages 8 and 9, still alternating with annoyance and fear. During the high piano sounds at the end, the singer may wish to stand, immobile, then slowly walk off during the decay of the cluster, as the lights go down. Stage should be totally dark by the start of the final glissando.

Much of the following material derives from the personal choices I made in my portrayal of the woman trapped overnight in a museum. Indulging in any opportunity for theatrics, I discovered a host of dramatic possibilities as I immersed myself in this exciting work.

The drama begins when darkness falls over the audience. Then, with slight stage illumination accompanied by glissandi, gongs, and *kecapi* in the introduction, the mood is set for the soprano's emergence from the shadows. On occasion, I have chosen to back onto the stage with spasmodic movements, snapping my head from side to side as if searching frantically for a familiar landmark. Most often, I have entered after the tape's second glissando, thus allowing the audience ample time to grasp the stark atmosphere and further highlighting the soprano's aloneness when she finally appears. After moving about the stage distractedly, I would stop at the bench, sit down slowly, as if in a trance, acknowledge my dilemma, and contemplate the situation while singing the opening phrase, "Who locked me..." During the C#-D#-E ostinato (see Example 9) on the words, "I wander among the fragments of gods, tarnished coins, embalmed gestures, chronologically arranged looking for the EXIT sign," I rose from the bench and staggered forward as if, disappointed by my failure to find an exit, I had settled for a half-hearted viewing of the museum's artifacts.

Since the decision lies with the performer, I decided to perceive the accompanying sound effects on the tape and the lengthy tape interpolations as antagonistic. In fact, I allowed the tape to take on the persona of my adversary, symbolizing the fear which gradually consumed me. Continuing after the *ostinato*, the plot thickens with loud, then soft drum sounds as the soprano speaks, "but in spite of the diagrams at every corner, labelled in red, YOU ARE HERE, the labyrinth holds me." Dramatically, I paralleled the disjunct melodic leaps and abrupt dynamic changes with panicked movements and demeanor (see Example 14).

Example 14: *A Night in the Royal Ontario Museum*, p. 2-3

A few seconds later, after some scene description, a thirty-second sound collage occurs. The collages can greatly enhance the drama if the singer wishes; they provide excellent opportunities for her to react dramatically to her situation and the taped sounds. Since Van de Vate gives no specific instructions, the singer may also choose to be totally oblivious to the taped sounds, thus creating another sort of drama. My choice, however, was to treat the sound collages as provocations to which I responded spontaneously.

Within seconds, the soprano stumbles upon the skeleton of a child. Here the tape's underlying collage rises and falls, as do the character's reactions to the sight. As I described this "skeleton child curled beside a clay pot and a few beads," I contorted and curled my body into a fetal position. My revulsion at the dead child served as motivation for my erratic behaviour during the next sound collage, when the audience witnessed the further unravelling of my mental state. I ran around the perimeter of the set in yet another futile attempt to locate an exit. Finding none, I threw myself on the floor at center stage behind the bench, on which, exhausted, I rested my head.

One phrase later, the soprano bumps into an exhibit where a button triggers a recorded voice. Terrified, she sings, "an idiot voice jogged by a pushed button," in another pictorial melodic line filled with leaps, accents, and staccati (see Example 15). This section is one of my favorite events in the drama, since the soprano is for the first time forced to hear the tape and publicly acknowledge what she hears.

Example 15: *A Night in the Royal Ontario Museum*, p. 6-7

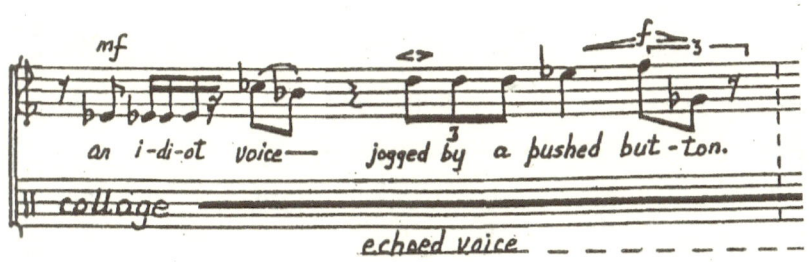

Van de Vate's above-the-staff setting of the ensuing text, "I am dragged to the mind's dead-end, the roar of the bone-yard," is extremely intense and catapults the drama to its climax (see Example 12). Though I have always chosen to sing rather than shout the text at the high pitch, intelligibility can prove difficult for the audience. Van de Vate rescues her performer with an optional lower octave followed by a spoken repetition of the text *ad libitum*. Since she ends this section with a weary, fragmented treatment of the text, I chose to follow the almost-shrieked melodic line as if hypnotized, with a weak, dazed facial expression.

As the woman falls deeper into madness, I demonstrated her broken spirit with a half-hearted portrayal of emotion from this point to the end of the piece. When the unrelenting, heartless museum responds to her last desperate plea for release with taunting slide whistles, I responded as though I welcomed the comic relief. I tilted my head, smiled broadly, opened my eyes wide, and led the final descending glissando into a crazed laugh. At the slide whistles' second entrance, I portrayed the character as totally mad, literally embracing the museum with outstretched arms, a cocked ear, a maniacal stare, and a psychotic grimace. Then, singing the final phrase in a very sweet, child-like voice, I assumed a fetal position on the bench and rocked back and forth, twisting a lock of hair.

As a performer, I particularly appreciate the adaptibility of *A Night in the Royal Ontario Museum*. Because the piece requires only one singer with recorded accompaniment, and the suggested staging and lighting are minimal (a simple spot for the soprano over a dim stage light, followed by darkness), it can be performed anywhere. Van de Vate offers no suggestions for costumes, so the soprano can choose to wear whatever she wishes; it is important, however, not to be encumbered with too many costume pieces or properties, since free movement about the stage is of key importance.

The set is almost nonexistent, except for the lighted red exit sign Van de Vate mentions in the preface, a backless bench, and the suggestion of a display case. I usually use the existing red exit signs in the auditorium and have encountered no logistical problems in doing so. Any type or size of backless bench can be used; I have, on occasion, even used a piano stool. Though a representation of a display case would be useful, it is certainly not necessary for a successful performance.

In part because of the minimal staging and lighting, the soprano must be able to captivate the audience dramatically, as well as musically. During the frequent taped sections when the soprano is tacet, movement and acting should never cease. By adding my own subplot to these taped sections, I have been able to keep the drama alive, and have made the performance more interesting both for myself and for the audience. On one occasion, I carried a brochure to represent a map of the museum, and spent time during the collages trying to orient myself.

The frequent pauses in the soprano's part, as well as the minimal staging instructions, allow the soloist a great deal of freedom. Although highly rewarding, this also requires much thought on her part; a shy or ill-planned performance will not be effective. There are nearly infinite creative possibilities for this piece; however, a lack of dramatic engagement is not one of them. The soloist must be an excellent actress as well as a fine singer.

CHAPTER THREE

Cocaine Lil

Profile of the Work

Van de Vate describes *Cocaine Lil*, a fifteen-minute work, as a "theater piece for mezzo soprano and four singers with percussion." The text is an anonymous American folk poem, to which the composer has added a few Latin words, many nonsense syllables, and much repetition. It may be divided into five sections, each based on the incident it describes.

PART A: SETTING THE SCENE

Did you ever hear about Cocaine Lil?
She lived in Cocaine town on Cocaine hill.
She had a cocaine dog and a cocaine cat,
They fought all night with the cocaine rat.

PART B: DESCRIBING LIL'S APPEARANCE

She had cocaine hair on her cocaine head.
She wore a snowbird hat and sleigh-riding clothes.
She had a cocaine dress that was poppy red.
On her coat she wore a crimson, cocaine rose.

PART C: TAKING A "COKE" TRIP

Big gold chariots on the Milky Way,
Snakes and elephants silver and gray,
O the cocaine blues they make me sad,
O the cocaine blues make me feel bad.

PART D: PAINTING THE PARTY SCENE

Lil went to a "snow" party one cold night,
And the way she sniffed was sure a fright.
There was Hophead Mag with Dopey Slim,
Kankakee Liz with Yen Shee Jim.

There was Hasheesh Nell and the Poppy Face Kid,
Climbed up snow ladders and down they slid;
There was Stepladder Kit, stood six feet,
And the Sleighriding Sisters are hard to beat.

PART E: IMMEDIATE ISOLATED EVENT

Along in the morning about half-past three
They were all lit up like a Christmas tree;
Lil got home and started to go to bed,
Took another "sniff" and it knocked her dead.

They laid her out in her cocaine clothes.
She wore a snowbird hat and a crimson rose;
On her headstone you'll find this refrain:
"She died as she lived, sniffing cocaine."

The text of *Cocaine Lil* differs from that of *A Night in the Royal Ontario Museum* in several ways. First, the character in *Night* speaks of her own experience in the first person, whereas the speaker in this poem narrates a story in third person. While *Night* is an evolving psychological drama tracing the mental disintegration of a character in free unrhymed verse, *Cocaine Lil* presents a narrative of scenes and events related in clear stanzas and rhymes. This more direct approach to the material, the more objective third-person narrator, and the poem's playful rhyme scheme lend *Cocaine Lil* a lighter, less serious character than the Atwood poem. While Atwood evokes considerable pathos for her deranged character, the anonymous author of *Lil* distances him/herself from the character and elicits little sympathy from the reader.

The author's use of colorful phrases (a "snowbird hat," the "poppy red" dress, the "crimson cocaine rose," etc.) adds to the poem's playful tone. The use of drug slang ("snow" for cocaine, "dope," "Poppy Face Kid," etc.) also adds to the somewhat light-hearted treatment of what could otherwise be construed as a tragic tale. Since *Lil* includes characters other than the addict herself, Van de Vate scores the piece for the main character and four additional singers who take on the roles of Lil's friends Hophead Mag, Dopey Slim, Kankakee Liz, and Yen Shee Jim.

Once again, Van de Vate works deftly with the text to create a world of colourful musical imagery. Her scoring, as well as her stage directions, suggest that she perceives the mezzo as Lil herself. This is especially clear in her setting of Part C, the "coke trip," and in the cadenza between Parts D and E. This cadenza, which serves as Van de Vate's detailed illustration of a cocaine trip, is replete with nonsense syllables and extended vocal techniques. The composer's decision to include four jazz/scat singers allows her to make more of the simple text, while fulfilling a number of dramatic functions; the vocalists serve variously as back-up singers, party friends of Lil, vocal percussionists, pallbearers, and narrators.

The opening page of the score (see Example 16) introduces a number of features that characterize the piece as a whole, including the absence of a time signature (though meter is suggested throughout), a predominantly atonal approach to pitch, frequent use of extended vocal techniques, polyphony, and aleatory. The predominantly conventional notation provides very precise instructions for dynamics, articulations, and tempi, though it yields at times to improvisation. As one would expect, the heaviest musical demands fall to the mezzo, whose part requires the ability to sing well in all ranges, with precise execution of rhythms, pitches, and articulations.

As with the pre-recorded accompaniment in *Night*, the accompaniment for *Lil*, provided by the jazz singers and percussion instruments, is an integral part of the piece. The jazz/scat singers particularly enrich the piece, both as accompaniment to Lil and as independent performers during interludes between Lil's entrances. Van de Vate confirms, however, that the singers' function is largely one of tone color. She never specifies their gender, but merely explains in the preface that, "Should actors rather than singers perform the ensemble part, they may wish to speak or chant all parts not specifically marked to be sung."

Example 16. *Cocaine Lil*, p. 1.

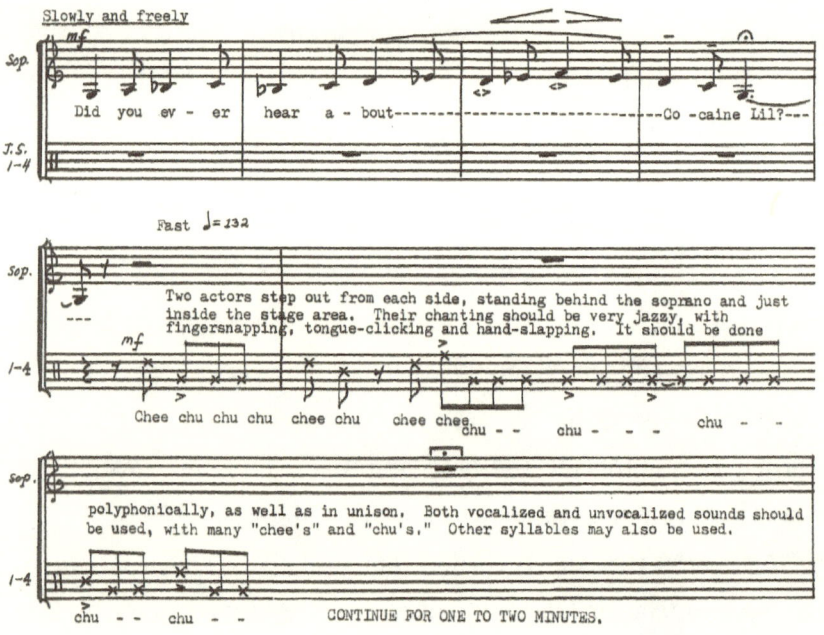

As the piece begins, the jazz singers adopt a subsidiary role of echo and accompaniment to Lil. As it progresses, however, the two forces become more equal until the vocal ensemble asserts its independence by presenting portions of the poem alone. In Part C, for instance, the singers leap to center stage shouting, "Snakes! Elephants!" then continue to improvise freely on the ensuing text, which depicts the coke trip. In the meantime, Lil sits with her head down as if asleep (see Example 17).

Example 17. *Cocaine Lil*, p. 7.

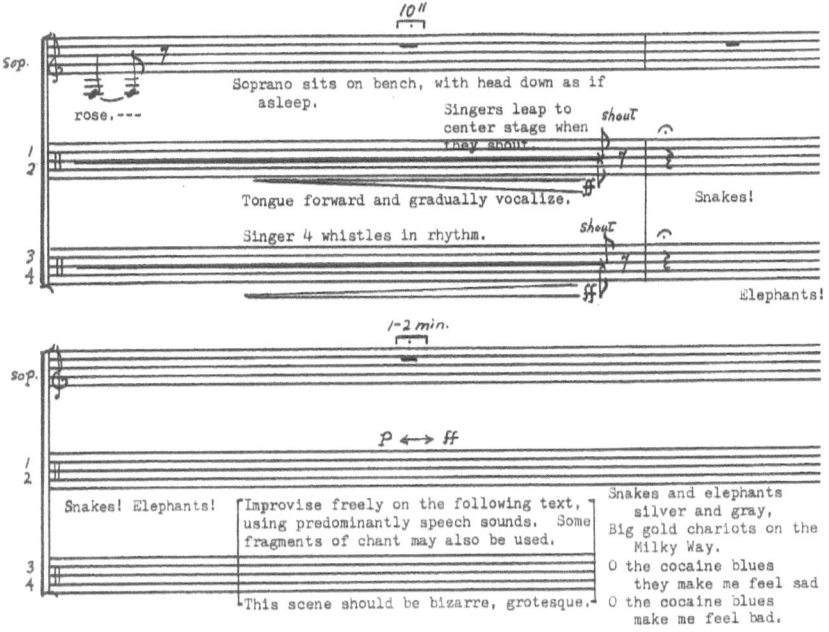

During the party scene in Part D, Lil and the ensemble alternate delivery of the text, with the ensemble frequently anticipating Lil's part. Van de Vate adapts the text to her musical purposes by frequently juggling words and phrases. The only exception to this text manipulation occurs midway through the piece, at the first stanza of Part E. Here, one ensemble member steps forward and recites the poem verbatim (see Example 18).

Example 18. *Cocaine Lil*, p. 16.

```
One singer steps forward and whispers or speaks (in dim light):
     "Along in the morning, about half-past three
      They were all lit up, like a Christmas tree;
      Lil got home and started to go to bed
      Took another 'sniff' ... "
All four singers speak slowly and emphatically:
     "and it knocked her dead."
```

The only non-vocal accompaniment in the piece occurs when the jazz singers take up percussion instruments, including a hand drum, claves, maracas, and sleigh bells. These percussion sounds, the ensemble's vocal prattle, and Lil's extended vocal techniques create such a cacophony that the lack of conventional instrumental accompaniment may at times go unnoticed.

Unlike that of *Night*, the opening of *Lil* is unaccompanied. Lil herself begins the work with a stark solo line sung in the chest register. After her first phrase, the jazz singers enter, chanting, finger-snapping, tongue-clicking, and hand-slapping. Van de Vate instructs that this "should be done polyphonically, as well as in unison." She adds, "Both vocalized and unvocalized sounds should be used, with many 'chee's' and 'chu's.' Other syllables may also be used." The polyphonic texture of the non-vocal sounds (finger-snapping, tongue-clicking, etc.) underneath the vocalized syllables creates an aural pandemonium, as well as a Stravinskyan motoric drive which lends the work a feeling of constant unrest.

Shortly after, Van de Vate requests an occasional meow or bark from the ensemble amid their carefully articulated gibberish. This odd assortment of unintelligible sounds widens the aesthetic distance between performer and audience, suggesting that Lil and her friends are in a drug-induced state of sub-human confusion. The staged drug trips give the audience a cold, dark, eerie feeling, only partially relieved by the detachment created by the third-person narrator.

Musical and Dramatic Flow

Like *A Night in the Royal Ontario Museum, Cocaine Lil* displays the composer's subtle, evocative treatment of text. Employing a myriad of characteristically Van de Vate special effects, she finds the perfect marriage between word and sound. With many timed sections and meticulous notation of rhythm, pitch, articulation, dynamics, and mood, Van de Vate leaves the performers with no unanswered questions.

At the beginning, Lil is alone onstage; the jazz singers only enter after her slow, free, opening phrase. At the ensemble's entrance, the tempo increases immediately to ♪=132 as the singers proceed to create a raucous backdrop for the forthcoming tale. The mezzo then intones Part A in a very simple, conjunct melody. The only word that Van de Vate draws special attention to is the last, "rat," on which she writes a preparatory descending glissando (see Example 19).

Example 19. *Cocaine Lil*, p. 4.

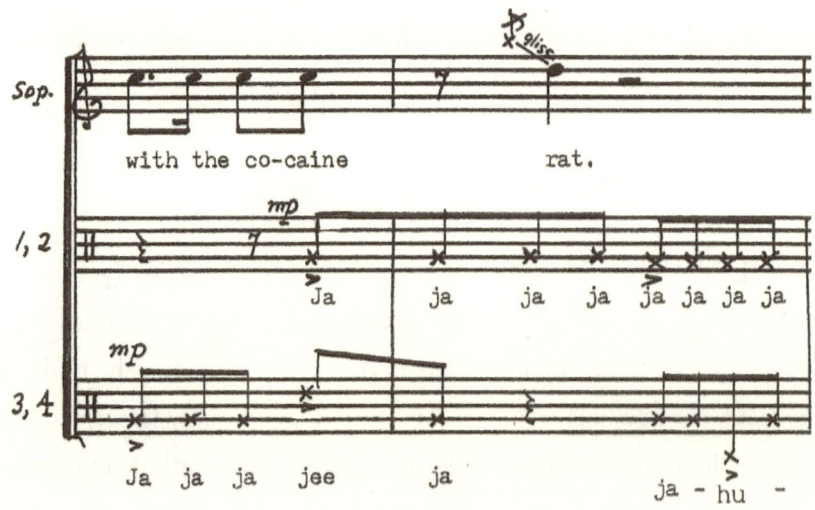

After the mezzo continues Part B over the ensemble's incessant babble, the jazz singers leap to center stage shouting "Snakes! Elephants!" (see Example 17). During this section, Van de Vate indicates that the ensemble should:

> Improvise freely on the following text, using predominantly speech sounds. Some fragments of chant may also be used. This scene should be bizarre, grotesque. As this scene winds down, the singers speak/chant increasingly slowly and softly. The lights go out gradually as the singers go back to the sides of the stage.

When the mezzo returns to the spotlight to sing Part D, which describes the "cocaine feast," she is to execute the notes "fast, jazzy, with finger-snapping," followed by a string of extended vocal techniques (see Example 20), which further stretch the distance between the real and surreal worlds. Immediately after, the ensemble assumes command of the text, chanting, "One cold night" five times at different pitches while Lil fades into an accompanying role, continuing the extended vocal techniques. The ensemble's text repetition, Lil's drug-induced outburst, the relentless tempo of "sempre ♩=100" and the added drums and claves all help to build excitement at the "snow" party.

Example 20. *Cocaine Lil*, p. 7-8.

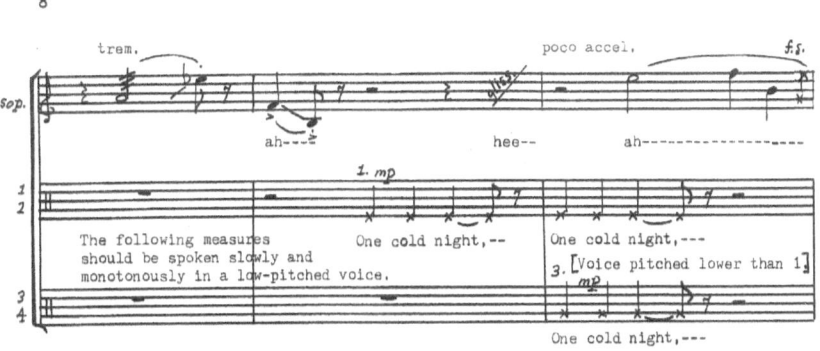

This section, which lasts for six full pages, is Stravinskian in its relentless rhythmic energy. The composer's consecutively higher pitched entrances on the word "climbed" offer an excellent example of text painting. When this section comes to an abrupt finish, Lil sings, "down they slid," dropping almost an octave and a half as the ensemble promptly ceases all sound (see Example 21).

Example 21. *Cocaine Lil*, p. 13.

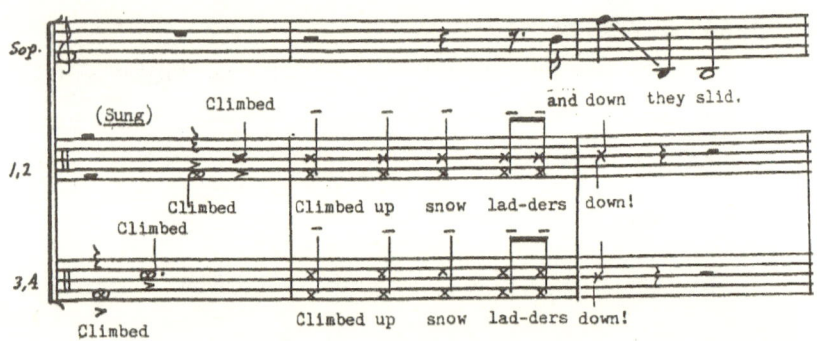

Lil continues for one last phrase, "O the cocaine blues," after which the ensemble moans during her sustained final note (see Example 22). This sets up her cadenza, which forms the heart of the piece. Saturated with unusual vocal techniques, strange vowel combinations, and leaps of nearly two octaves, the cadenza depicts Lil's ride through the "snow." Though the cadenza is unmetered, Van de Vate includes specific pitches, rhythms, articulations, and dynamics (see Example 23).

Example 22. *Cocaine Lil,* p. 27.

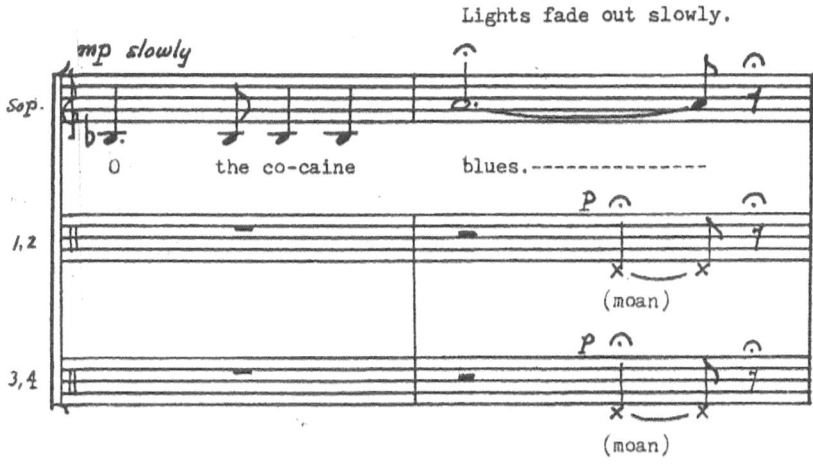

The mezzo performing Lil must have a strong vocal technique in all registers to perform this cadenza without harming her voice. On the more than dozen leaps of over an octave, the soprano's voice moves acrobatically between head and chest registers. At the cadenza's conclusion, Lil sings a chromatic scale ending abruptly on a high B-flat, a minor sixth above the slow trill which follows the chromatic scale shown in the example.

Example 23. *Cocaine Lil*, p. 14-15

Part E becomes a monologue for one of the ensemble singers, as Van de Vate indicates: "One singer steps forward and whispers or speaks (in dim light)." The others join in the last unison phrase, "and it knocked her dead." This announcement of Lil's death is answered by two seconds of mocking sleigh bells. The stage is in total darkness as Lil whispers "dead" from the rear. As the stage again becomes illuminated, the mezzo intones, "O Domine, Domine Patri O Morte" in a Gregorian chant style. The composer's descending glissando on a flutter at the words "O Morte" adds an interesting, rather macabre touch. (see Example 24).

Example 24. *Cocaine Lil*, p. 16.

Lil and the ensemble continue to sing, "knocked her dead." Then she executes a quirky, almost comical melody on a descending major seventh followed by an ascending tritone (see Example 24). To this strange little tune Van de Vate adds highly precise staccato and marcato articulations. The ensemble chants a rhythmic ostinato ♪♩ on the text "knocked her dead," while the mezzo's melody evolves into a legato, siren-like swoop culminating in a high fortissimo shriek. All of these effects combine to convey the horror of death by drug overdose (see Example 25).

Example 25. *Cocaine Lil*, p. 17.

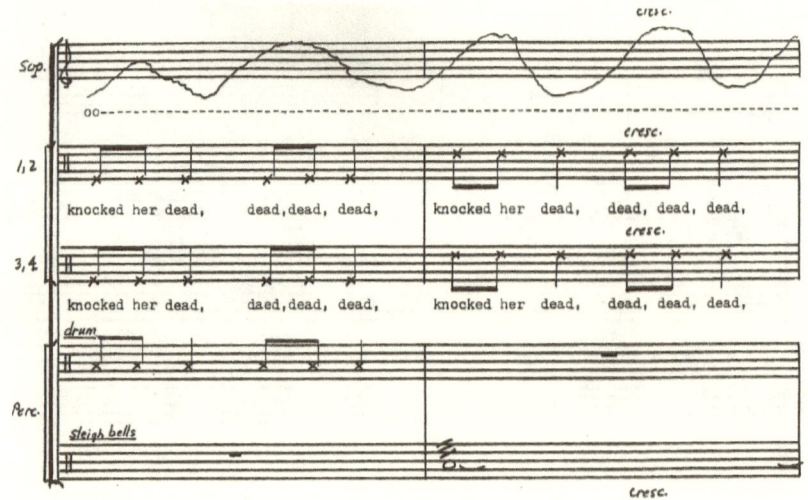

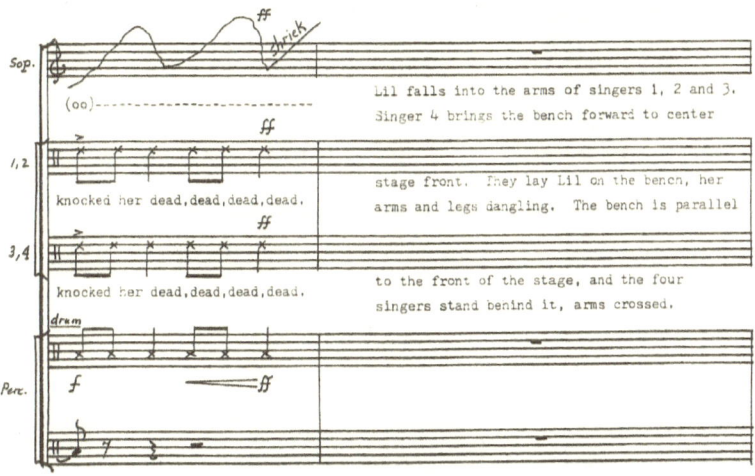

Lil falls into the singers' arms, and her corpse is displayed on the bench parallel to the stage. The four singers cross their arms, stand behind the bench, and sing the theme from Chopin's "Marche funèbre" (the third movement of the Piano Sonata in B-flat Minor, Op. 35) with the words, "They laid her out in her cocaine clothes" to percussion accompaniment (see Example 26).

Example 26. *Cocaine Lil*, p. 19.

As the piece approaches its close, Lil sings another quirky tune with leaps of a major seventh and a minor ninth. Set to the text, "on her head-stone you will find," the mezzo seems to be stepping out of Lil's character, taunting the drug addict as if to say, "you make your bed, you lie in it, Lil." At the end of this phrase, the mezzo is instructed to drop her voice quickly, almost two full octaves (see Example 27).

Example 27. *Cocaine Lil*, p. 23.

In the final pages, while the mezzo sings variations on Chopin's "Marche funèbre," the ensemble engages in much contrapuntal interplay to create an ever-intensifying cacophony, which relaxes only on the penultimate page. After a grand pause six bars before the end, the jazz singers paint the text with a long descending glissando on their last phrase, "And it knocked her dead!" Lil's death is tolled with eerie levity on the sleigh bells, and the lights are suddenly extinguished. Out of the darkness, we hear Lil reiterate the familiar tune used just before her cadenza on the text, "O the cocaine blues" (see Example 28).

Example 28. *Cocaine Lil*, p. 27.

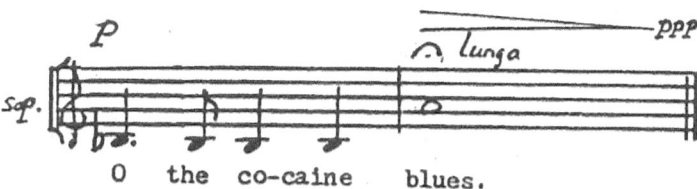

Performance Considerations

Cocaine Lil has a much more involved narrative than *A Night in the Royal Ontario Museum*. Since the dramatic and musical events are more complicated, Van de Vate offers many blocking instructions. She is, however, careful to allow performers a degree of artistic license, going so far as to state that pitches and rhythms may be approximate. This allows for a great deal of flexibility, particularly with respect to the duration of the piece; recordings of the work range from eleven to fifteen minutes. In the preface to the piece, the composer outlines her open attitude:

> *Cocaine Lil* may be performed as concert music or as a theater piece with simple staging and action. Some suggestions for the latter are indicated in the score. They are not definitive, and other versions are certainly possible.
>
> Percussion, which may be entirely hand-held, includes the following instruments: medium-sized drum

(tom-tom), claves, one maraca or afuche, and sleigh bells.

No special percussion techniques are required since the parts are very simple.

Pronunciation is phonetic in English.

Repetition of syllables is sometimes represented by a single dash under a note – for example, chu-- = chu chu chu.

Abbreviations include: f.s. = finger snap and h.c. = hand clap.

X-notes may be chanted, sung, performed as *Sprechstimme* or spoken. Relative pitch levels are indicated by staff placement. Performers may exercise considerable freedom in interpreting the parts; they may wish to speak or chant all parts not specifically marked to be sung.

In preparing the piece, participants might wish to approach it as an exercise in counting and coordination. The work is carefully crafted, all of its ingredients coordinated in perfect syntax, but challenges physical coordination as well as mental faculties. For example, halfway through the piece, the ensemble incorporates three percussion instruments into an already complex rhythmic texture (see Example 29).

Example 29. *Cocaine Lil*, p. 11.

Then five pages from the end, nonsense syllables are woven into the fabric of hand-claps, drums, claves, and sleigh bells, creating even greater chaos (see Example 30).

Example 30. *Cocaine Lil*, p. 22.

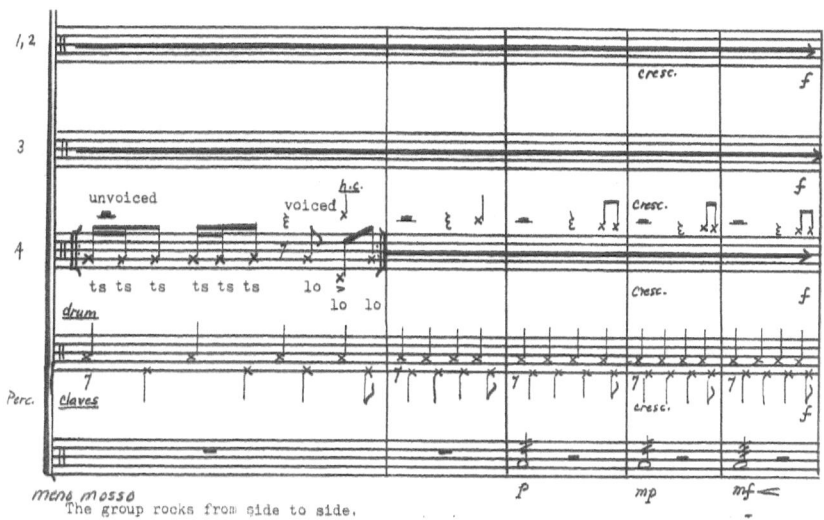

The incorporation of the mezzo part into the complicated ensemble texture adds yet another dimension which requires a great deal of rehearsal time. While using a recording of the accompanying ensemble parts might make rehearsing somewhat simpler, it would also add new challenges because of its inflexibility. On the other hand, a recorded accompaniment would probably increase the number of performances of this extraordinary work and help it gain the audience it deserves.

Unlike *Night*, *Cocaine Lil* contains just a few timed sections, and most appear early in the work. In the passage from Example 31, Van de Vate assigns a time limit to one of her many aleatory sections. Most of the aleatory passages, are not durationally restricted, however, thus giving the performer considerable freedom. They often consist of improvisation on pitches and nonsense syllables (see Example 31).

Example 31. *Cocaine Lil*, p. 4.

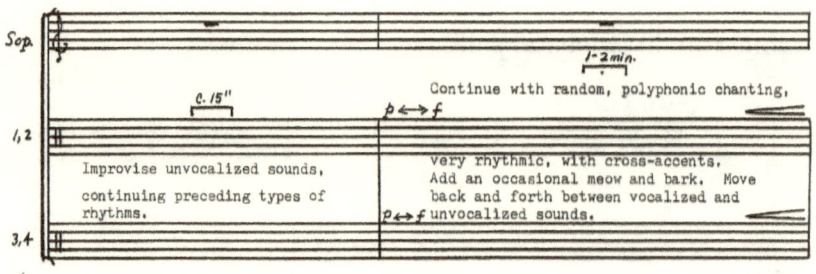

In another typical example of the composer's aleatory scoring (see Example 32), even greater freedom is given, since there is no metric or pitch structure, but merely a one- to two-minute time limit.

Example 32. *Cocaine Lil*, p. 7.

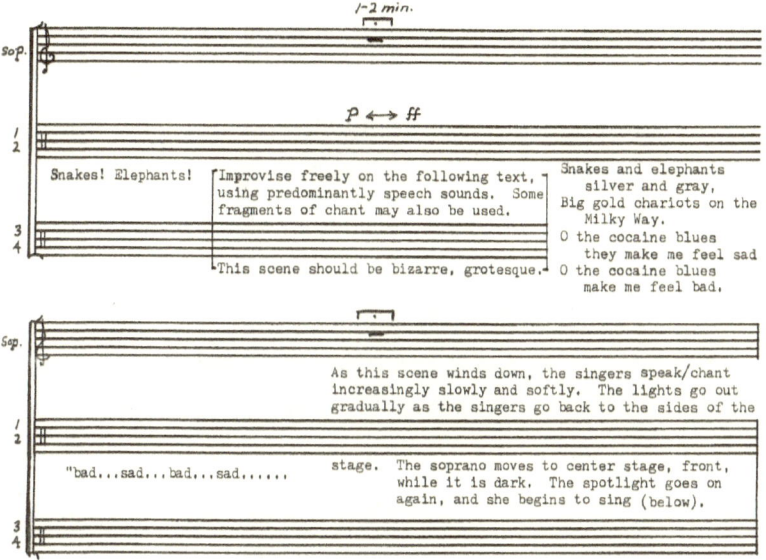

Although Van de Vate is generally meticulous in her notation of rhythms and pitches, she frequently allows the performer to make her own choices, particularly in the case of blocking. For example, during the cadenza, the singer may "walk around or sit down on the bench part of the time." Nonetheless, Van de Vate makes her conception of the piece quite clear. Her brief description of the scene and character at the opening is rather specific, providing a point of departure for the performer's own creative additions.

> The stage or performance area is rather small, and there is a backless bench to one side. The soprano walks slowly and carelessly to center stage. She wears a bright red dress which hangs unevenly, its V-neck carelessly draped. She is sloppy and looks dissolute. She begins to sing in a husky ("torchy") voice, not looking directly at the audience. The lights are dim.

Logistically, the requirements are the same as those of *Night* –
minimal lighting, simple costumes, and few properties or set pieces.
There should be a spotlight in addition to the regular lighting panel.
The lights never fully illuminate the stage, but change often from
darkness to dim light or to spotlighting.

Concerning costumes, Van de Vate suggests that the mezzo
wear "a bright red dress which hangs unevenly, its V-neck carelessly
draped." No costumes are specified for the jazz singers, and there are
no props except the backless bench.

In her brief preface, the composer mentions that "the stage or
performance area is rather small." A variation of stage space would
not present a problem, however. An usually effective performance
by the Music Academy in Katowice, Poland, set *Cocaine Lil* in the
tunnels of a sewer. Van de Vate applauded this choice, which opened
up entirely new possibilities for the work.

CHAPTER FOUR

In the Shadow of the Glen

Profile of the Work

The chamber opera *In the Shadow of the Glen* employs a libretto adapted by the composer from a play by John Millington Synge. This 42-minute work is set in rural Ireland around 1900, and all of the action occurs over the course of one stormy night in a small cottage – "the last cottage at the head of a long glen." The cast includes four characters: Nora Burke, a mezzo-soprano; her husband, Dan Burke, a tenor; a young herdsman, Michael, a baritone; and a nameless tramp, also a tenor. Van de Vate summarizes the story in an opening note:

> Although there are many elements of comedy in the opera, it is essentially the poignant story of a poor woman who lived a lonely life in rural Ireland around 1900 and occasionally talked with the men who passed by her cottage. Misunderstood by her old and unkind husband, she is tricked by him into looking forward to a better life after his death. In ultimately forcing her to leave, he consigns her to a humiliating life of hardship in the local poorhouse or an even harder life walking

the roads. Synge's play was violently criticized in its day for its unflattering depiction of Irish family life.

A more detailed plot summary is given here to aid the reader's understanding in the ensuing discussion.

Plot Summary

Nora Burke is alone on a stormy night around the turn of the century in the last cottage at the head of a long glen in County Wicklow, Ireland. Her husband has just died and his body is lying on a bed against the wall, covered with a sheet.

A knock is heard, and Nora answers the door. A tramp, seeking a place to sleep, looks past her and sees the body. Nora asks him to come in out of the rain anyway, and he accepts. She pours him a glass of whiskey, gives him a pipe and tobacco, and they begin to talk. She tells him what an unpleasant old man her husband had been and asks if he had seen a young man with a herd of mountain ewes. He tells her that he did.

Nora asks the tramp to stay with the body, while she goes to find the young man, who had sometimes worked for her and her husband. The tramp offers to go in her place, but she insists he could not find his way in the rain and leaves him alone.

The sheet on the bed is pulled slowly down, and Dan Burke looks out. He tells the terrified tramp he is not really dead and pours himself some whiskey. He takes a stick from the cupboard and says that he has a bad wife. Voices are heard outside, and Dan Burke lies back on the bed, covering himself with the sheet. Nora enters with Michael, the young herdsman.

The tramp goes to sleep by the chimney, and Nora sits down at the table with Michael. She puts a stocking of money on the table, and she and Michael begin to count it. They discuss getting married; Dan Burke sits up noiselessly from under the sheet, but they do not hear him. He sneezes violently. Michael tries to get to the door, but Dan puts his back against it, the stick in his hand. He tells Nora she must leave immediately.

The tramp tries to intercede on her behalf, knowing that for Nora to leave would mean certain death from destitution and starvation. Nora looks at Michael, who timidly suggests the workhouse in Rathdrum. Dan tells the tramp to leave with Nora, who stands shaking with silent sobs. The kindly tramp says he will take Nora with him and that he will show her how to care for herself out on the road. They leave, and Michael attempts to slink out after them. Dan invites him to come back for a glass of whiskey, and toasts his health. They raise their glasses and Dan can still be heard laughing after the curtain closes.

The libretto is peppered with somewhat convoluted Irish turns of phrase, which can seem a bit foreign to today's performers and listeners. For example, in the beginning, Nora tells the tramp that she has "no turf drawn for the winter." Later on, the tramp confronts Dan's feigned death by saying, "It's not for nothing you're making out to be dead." These linguistic peculiarities are at once lyrical and confusing; one of the most quaintly cryptic utterances occurs near the end of the opera, when Nora sings, "It's a queer thing to see an old man sitting there in his bed, with no teeth in him, and a rough word in his mouth, and his chin the way it would take the bark from the edge of an oak board you'd use in building a door."

These colloquialisms also help establish the opera's setting. Surely any reader can envision a rugged country life when Nora asks the herdsman, Michael, "How would I live and I an old woman, if I didn't marry a man with a bit of farm and sheep back on the hills?" What would today be seen as the rampant sexism of the text further colors the story's sense of time and place. Dan's response to the tramp's concern for Nora's future (if he "puts her out on the road") is one such instance.

> Let her walk round below and beg money at the crossroads, or sell her songs to the men. Walk out now, Nora, and you'll soon be getting old with that life; soon your teeth will fall and your head will be like a bush where sheep do leap a gap.

Perhaps the ultimate sexist blow occurs at the very end, when Dan invites Michael to join him for whiskey after throwing Nora out of the house into the cold, stormy night. Instead of defending her, Michael celebrates with Dan, toasting, "God reward you." Laughing, they drink to each other's health as the curtain closes.

For practical reasons, the entire libretto will not be printed here, nor will the opera's complete psychological flow be traced as with the two foregoing works. In general terms, however, the primary conflict involves a lonely and unhappy housewife who yearns to escape the drudgery of her life, and her old, suspicious husband who is trying to trap her into revealing that she is unfaithful. The story's climax occurs when Dan Burke's death hoax is shattered by a vigorous sneeze from beneath his bedsheet shroud. Anyone who has seen Puccini's *Gianni Schicchi* will recall a similar scene in which the trickster, Gianni Schicchi, disguised as Buoso Donati, executes a selfish ruse from a "deathbed." *Shadow* finds its resolution when Nora resigns herself to a life on the road with the tramp.

Van de Vate presents the text in a very straightforward manner, with little deviation from the conversational format of the play. The text is set syllabically and includes several spoken lines. Wisely, the composer allows the text's natural flow to influence the musical parameters of melody and rhythm. Important syllables and words fall on strong beats, and high and/or long-held notes provide for greater intelligibility of the lyrics. This idiomatic textual treatment allows the singers considerable musical and dramatic flexibility.

For this one-act opera, the composer has chosen a small ensemble with typical chamber orchestra instrumentation: two flutes, two oboes, two clarinets, two bassoons, two horns, bass trombone, harp, strings, and percussion. The bass trombone's occasional contributions seem largely reserved for text painting and comedic effect. Similarly, the rather extensive percussion section, with hosts of timbral possibilities, responds to moments of levity throughout the opera. Two percussionists are responsible for glockenspiel, xylophone, marimba, chimes, tam-tam, 5 temple blocks, timpani, snare drum, bass drum, medium tom-tom, tenor drum, medium and large suspended cymbals, crash cymbals, small, medium, and large wood blocks, medium and large triangle, guiro, cabasa, ratchet, and whip. Van de Vate uses this varied collection of instruments to punctuate dramatic gestures and create special effects. In the short orchestral introduction, for instance, the xylophone doubles the viola's playful melody just as the tramp's first knock on the door is heard (see Example 33).

Example 33. *In the Shadow of the Glen*, mm. 12-16, p. 3.

Shortly after, as Nora describes how Dan died, the dramatic suspense is heightened by a suspended cymbal roll and a jauntily disjunct bass clarinet line (see Example 34).

Example 34. *In the Shadow of the Glen*, mm. 96-98.

Later, Nora sings to the tramp, "You wouldn't find your way.... There is a small path only which runs between two brooks where a mule and a cart will be drowned" to the accompaniment of an improvising marimbist. Her instructions to "improvise in middle register, using 16th or shorter note values" and not to "blend with orchestral harmonies," parallel the very confusing, almost dangerous journey Nora is about to take (see Example 35).

Example 35. *In the Shadow of the Glen*, mm 198-206.

Further examples of text painting and other mood-setting orchestral interjections will be explored later.

The orchestra opens the work with a 22-bar introduction; there is no overture. During this introduction, the texture is often sparse, but the comic mood is set with animated, disjunct tunes and off-kilter, syncopated rhythms. Pizzicato strings, abrupt and frequent dynamic shifts, accents, *marcati*, and exceptional colors from the percussion section create an appropriate atmosphere for the unfolding of the drama. Van de Vate's penchant for diversity of tone color emerges in these initial measures, where she employs seven of the twenty percussion instruments. The prominence of percussion so early in the opera foreshadows its later importance. The curtain rises after ten measures. Three bars later, the action begins with the tramp's first knock at the cottage door, then the sung dialogue begins.

Glancing at the score's first page, we see that this is a tonal work with conventional notation. Van de Vate herself confirms that it is "modal and diatonic, predominantly triadic[11]." The first two 4/4 measures, marked lento, consist of a loud, closely spaced, four-note chord for seven winds and lower strings. Under this heavy sound, timpani and string basses play a menacing tremolo, while the tam-tam rolls for a full nine bars, suggesting impending drama. This foreboding chord diminishes from *ff* to *ppp* and is followed by a spritely unison melody played pizzicato in the violins and violas. The initial juxtaposition of tragedy and comedy returns throughout the opera and represents one of the work's primary conflicts.

---

[11]   Nancy Van de Vate, interview by Michelle Vought, August 1, 1993, tape recording, Vienna, Austria

Example 36. *In the Shadow of the Glen*, mm. 1-6.

IN THE SHADOW OF THE GLEN

Cottage kitchen; turf fire on the right; a bed near it against the wall with a body lying on it covered with a sheet. A door is at the other end of the room, with a low table near it, and stools, or wooden chairs. There are a couple of glasses on the table, and a bottle of whiskey, as if for a wake, with two cups, a teapot, and a home-made cake. There is another small door near the bed. Nora Burke is moving about the room, settling a few things, and lighting candles on the table, looking now and then at the bed with an uneasy look. Someone knocks softly at the door. She takes up a stocking with money from the table and puts it in her pocket. Then she opens the door.

Nancy Van de Vate
1960/1994

As in the two theater pieces previously discussed, the instrumental part in this work is by no means mere accompaniment, but rather an equal partner in the creation of dramatic sound. Treating every member of the orchestra (including the percussion) as another character in the story, she reserves each one's use for specific lyrics or dramatic events. Because of the orchestra's independent participation, which often creates complex counterpoints, singers who perform this work must possess strong rhythmic and aural skills.

Much of the vocal line is recitative-like, a result of the composer's conversational setting of the text. However, there is no traditional recitative/aria structure, nor is there a clearly defined division of sections within the opera. Each musical event flows directly into the next, and the drama is never allowed to slacken. The orchestral texture is often very sparse when the characters are singing. The instruments of the ensemble comment on the action with brief rhythmic interjections and animated musical gestures between sections of sung or spoken dialogue. Sometimes these flourishes elide with the ensuing vocal lines, and sometimes they accompany movement or a specific stage action. An excellent example is when the tramp fills one of Dan's pipes, offered to him by Nora, to the accompaniment of timpani, xylophone, English horn, and strings (see Example 37).

Example 37. *In the Shadow of the Glen*, mm. 109-114, p. 20.

The power of the full orchestra is reserved for highly dramatic moments, as when Nora explains how Dan died (see Example 34), and at the climax of the opera, where Dan spoils his ruse by sneezing violently (see Example 38).

Set in strict dialogue with no extraneous music, the piece only becomes vocally dense on the two occasions when two or more people sing simultaneously. Halfway through the opera, the tramp, Nora, and Michael begin a trio, which is reduced to a short-lived duet between Nora and Michael just half a minute later. The only other vocal ensemble occurs toward the end, where the tramp tries to convince Nora that life on the road will not be so bad. Mirroring the earlier ensemble piece, the traitorous Michael makes the duet a trio by reiterating the tramp's text. As the trio fades, Dan commands Nora to "Get out of that door!" and the sparse musical texture returns.

As in most Van de Vate compositions, timbre is paramount, and her colorful orchestration produces a myriad of interesting sounds that conjure up mood, evoke atmosphere, and create an exciting theatrical experience.

Example 38. *In the Shadow of the Glen*, mm. 498-500, p. 75.

In the ensuing seventeen measures, the composer sets up the action with disjunct, rhythmic string melodies interrupted by xylophone and temple blocks, under which cello and bass tremolos build suspense. Finally, in the last five bars of the introduction, all the instruments except the brass strike another dissonant fortissimo chord and continue unison in an agitated rhythm to the final dissonant chord marked *sffz > pp* (see Example 39).

Example 39. *In the Shadow of the Glen*, mm. 17-22.

Even without the rising curtain, the set, and the two loud knocks on the door (all of which occur during the introduction), the music alone creates a sense of high drama. Following a harp chord, the tramp's voice is the first to be heard. He is answered immediately by Nora, who laments her loneliness to the tramp: "How would you, passing in the dark night, know how lonely, how lonely this house is with no near neighbor at all?" (see Example 40). The orchestration here is but a thin shadow of her lyrics, reflecting her lack of companionship.

This lonely, stark mood is paralleled by a sudden offbeat stroke on the snare drum (snares off) and a few pizzicato notes in the low strings.

Example 40. *In the Shadow of the Glen*, m. 136-139.

Musical and Dramatic Flow

Van de Vate's dramatic tendencies and textual deftness are especially suited to the operatic genre. Though she does not use leitmotifs as such, there are several recurring themes, the first being a spritely string melody in measure three (see Example 36). This three-bar tune reappears in the same form and instrumentation 36 pages later, before the tramp launches into the "De Profundis" intoned in response to Dan's supposed death. Variations of the same melody resurface on two occasions: first, toward the end of the work, when Dan throws Nora out of the house, and later, when she gathers her belongings into her shawl as she prepares to depart. The tune is never sung, but always accompanies spoken dialogue or action.

A second theme is introduced midway through the piece, when the tramp falls asleep after Nora and Michael's return to the cottage. Fittingly, this theme resembles Brahms' "Wiegenlied" with its ascending minor third on a similar rhythm. That same minor third motif recurs in transposition in the course of the next few pages, then disappears for 70 measures until Nora exclaims to Michael, "Why would I marry you?" This time, it is played a half-step lower than the original, but continues to be heard in its exact rhythm in the orchestra for a full 20 measures. Like the first theme, this second is found mostly in the orchestra.

Van de Vate further defines the characters by assigning to them distinct melodic styles and instrumentations. Nora's part, the most lyrical of the four, is frequently accompanied by flute and harp, and her line is often reinforced in the flute or violin. In contrast, Dan's static, monotonous melodies reflect his flat, soulless character. His conjunct lines sound more spoken than sung, except for the occasional abrupt leap. Unlike Nora, Dan is given no distinctive orchestration; the ensemble merely interjects an occasional note or chord to punctuate his vocal lines.

Discussion of the orchestral depiction of text and drama will be illustrated with several outstanding examples. At the beginning of the story, Nora describes Dan's demise to the tramp, saying, "...he made a great leap and let out a great cry." She intones this fatal account to the accompaniment of disorienting, leaping melodies found in the clarinet, harp, and cello, while the trombone and French horn offer an ascending countermelody to her final phrase, "and let out a great cry." All screeches to a fortissimo halt on the last word, "cry" (see Example 34).

Later, when Nora goes to seek help, leaving the tramp alone with Dan's body, the tenor speaks the "De Profundis" in Latin while low strings, bassoon, and timpani provide an austere, drone-like accompaniment. Van de Vate anticipates Dan's revelation by intensifying the suspense with a bowed tremolo in the basses and a quirky reiteration of the theme from measure 3, played pizzicato in the high strings. Van de Vate slowly builds up the orchestration with a Hitchcock-like knack for suspense, eventually climbing to a fortissimo clash by the full orchestra, with melodies outlining tritones in several keys as the tramp springs to his feet in terror (see Example 41).

Example 41. *In the Shadow of the Glen*, mm. 225-236.

Michelle Vought

80

In several cases, Van de Vate highlights isolated words and phrases through orchestral timbre. Dan describes the physical discomfort of his prolonged prone state to the tramp as he sings, "…and there's been the devil's own fly itching my nose." Oboes, clarinets, and high strings (in pizzicato) interpolate an accented eighth-note on "fly" to depict Dan's miniscule torturer. Later, as Michael laments the recalcitrance of his sheep, singing, "They ran off into one man's oats and another man's hay, and tumbling, tumbling into the red bogs, till it's more like a pack of old goats than sheep they were," Van de Vate accentuates the words "ran" and "tumbling" with descending sixteenth-note scales in 9/8 time. Immediately after Dan's climactic sneeze, he threatens Michael: "You'll not marry her while I'm rotting in the Seven Churches, and you'll see the thing I'll give you will follow you on the back mountain when the wind is high." A derisive whip cracks in the percussion section upon the word "rotting."

Dan continues to condemn Nora with his gruesome predictions:

It's on lonesome roads she'll go, and hide herself away until the end will come and they find her stretched like a dead sheep, with the frost on her, or the big spiders maybe, and they put their webs on her, in the butt of a ditch.

Van de Vate paints this dreadful picture with a cymbal crash on the word "stretched," a suspended cymbal roll on "frost," an intervening whip on a rest, and a sudden eighth-note marked *fp* in piccolo and flute on the word "spiders." She sets the final phrase of this macabre scene to pedal tones in the low winds and trombone (see Example 42).

Perhaps Van de Vate's most comical use of text painting occurs during the tramp's final solo, when, in an attempt to comfort Nora, he sings, "…and there'll be no old fellow wheezing like a sick sheep, close to your ear." Here, the composer assigns the role of the wheezing sheep to the guiro.

Example 42. *In the Shadow of the Glen*, mm. 547-555.

Performance Considerations

This chamber opera was first premiered with piano in 1999, then with orchestra in 2010 at the Longy School of Music in Cambridge, Massachusetts. Given the complexity of the music, with its intricately woven orchestral and vocal parts, and the complex psychologies of the characters, the work must be prepared with the same care as a full-scale opera. The orchestra fulfills several roles, at times interjecting brief and sudden flourishes and fanfares, at other times providing accompaniment for action (such as lighting a pipe or leaving a room), and finally interacting with the vocal lines through animated countermelodies. This work is a challenge for all involved, aurally, rhythmically, vocally, and dramatically. Fortunately for the singers, however, Van de Vate's piece is not atonal, but modal and diatonic and predominantly triadic. Delivery and intelligibility of text should not present a problem, since the setting adheres quite closely to the lilt and cadence of an Irish brogue, and the orchestra's often sparse texture allows the words to be heard. Since the opera is set mainly in dialogue, with few arias as showcases for vocal virtuosity, singers should approach it as an ensemble work. Vocal lines often enter on each other's heels, with no prearranged moments for reorganization if problems arise in synchronization. With no single performer taking the lead and roughly equal amounts of solo singing for all four performers, ensemble rehearsals are mandatory for this tightly knit work.

While idiomatic, the vocal parts are highly demanding, requiring all four singers to use their full ranges in executing Van de Vate's disjunct melodies. Though the role of Nora is scored for a mezzo, she should have a solid high C. Dan, a tenor, must be capable of a good high B, and Michael, the baritone, must successfully negotiate a high F#. The abrupt and dramatic leaps render these roles best suited to heavier, more dramatic voices.

To present the best possible production, singers should not only be excellent musicians but extraordinary actors. The rather static plot, which depends largely on conversation--except, of course, for the trickster Dan's contribution-- results in a great deal of what singers refer to as "standing and singing." This lack of physical action must be compensated for by in-depth character development and stage presence, requiring considerable acting skill.

Van de Vate includes many stage directions throughout the score, all easily accomplished without sacrificing good vocal production. Unlike *Night* and *Lil*, *Shadow* is a straightforward drama and not as much an atmospheric, effect-filled piece. The earlier pieces rely heavily on effects produced by spotlights and other mood lighting to evoke an eerie atmosphere as important as the unfolding drama. The evocation of these uncanny moods increases the distance between performer and listener. *Shadow*, though more separated from the present in terms of setting, engages the audience more directly, allowing them to peer through a cottage window in 1900 rural Ireland. The following describes the stage at the beginning of the opera; it remains the same throughout the piece.

> Cottage kitchen; turf fire on the right; a bed near it against the wall with a body lying on it covered with a sheet. A door is at the other end of the room, with a low table near it, and stools, or wooden chairs. There are a couple of glasses on the table, and a bottle of whiskey, as if for a wake, with two cups, a teapot, and a home-made cake. There is another small door near the bed. Nora Burke is moving about the room, setting a few things, and lighting candles on the table, looking now and then at the bed with an uneasy look. Someone knocks softly at the door. She takes up a stocking with money from the table and puts it in her pocket. Then she opens the door.

The costumes, set, and properties are understandably more elaborate in this piece than in the previously discussed works. Van de Vate gives no instructions concerning costumes, but since the characters live in poverty, simple but shabby farm clothing should suffice. The set and its properties pose greater challenges, since the list of properties is substantial. A small technical staff of set designer and properties manager may be necessary for a successful production.

CHAPTER FIVE

Nemo: Jenseits von Vulkania

Profile of the Work

On the title page, this German-language opera is referred to as "eine romantische Märchenoper in vier Akten," or "a romantic fairy-tale opera in four acts." Allen Cortès, who commissioned the opera, was also the librettist, and his work was inspired by Jules Verne's fantastical adventure novel, *20,000 Leagues under the Sea*.

Van de Vate says that *Nemo* contains many familiar operatic conventions, with a few extras thrown in for good measure: a Turkish belly dance, a Polynesian song of thanksgiving, and fireworks, for example. These "extras" were the librettist's idea and reflected his wish to keep the opera entertaining to the general public. Conceived in the same spirit as Mozart's *Die Zauberflöte*, the work is meant to be fun and in the librettist's own words, "to send the audience home whistling the tunes."

Van de Vate worked intensively on adapting the libretto, which was initially far too long. A cast list, plot, and detailed scene synopsis follow.

DIE PERSONEN

NEMO	Kommandeur des U-Bootes "Nautilus," Sohn des berühmten Kapitan Nemo	Tenor
ELENA	Tochter des gefallenen Hauptmannes der Kolonialwache	Sopran
DANNOSO	Herrscher von Meeresland	Bass
FRANZ	Kapitän des Handelsdampfschiffes "Eisenhut"	Bariton
MUTTER	Mutter der Elena	Alt

Admiral der Meeresland-Flotte	Bariton
3 Minister Dannosos	Bass/Tenor/ Bariton
Knabe des Fischervolks	Knabensopran
Seemöwe	Sopran
Nachtwächter von Meeresland	Bass
Alanya	Bauchtänzerin
Meeresländer Volk	Chor
Fischervolk der Insel Katharina	Chor
Matrosen des Schiffes "Eisenhut"	Männerchor
Grottenmannschaft/Aquanauten der "Nautilus"	Männerchor
Dannoso'sche Leibwache	Statisten
Matrosen und Offiziere des Meeresländer Kriegsschiffes	Statisten

PLOT SUMMARY

The opera takes place somewhere in the South Seas around 1900. Commander Nemo, son of the builder of the Nautilus, the submarine that traveled 20,000 leagues under the sea in Jules Verne's novel, has taken over his father's scientific work and command of the Nautilus. When not traveling deep in the ocean, the submarine and its crew are at rest in the undersea grotto of Vulkania.

Twenty years earlier, a bloody coup had displaced the European colonial administration of Meeresland, a large island in the South Seas, and the evil Dannoso had installed himself as dictator. The head of the former colonial administration was killed, and his wife and infant daughter, Elena, fled to Katherina Island, where they lived peacefully among the natives. Franz, then also very young, was taken aboard the Nautilus, where he and the son of Captain Nemo grew up together. Franz later returned to the world above and is now captain of a trading vessel that sometimes visits Meeresland.

The younger Nemo has briefly visited Katherina, and he and Elena have fallen in love. However his world is one only of men, and Elena can never share it. In the meantime, Dannoso, who has ruled for twenty years, has become concerned about the succession of his power. He decides to marry Elena, who is reputed to be a very beautiful young woman.

ACT ONE

SCENE ONE: Meeresland, near daybreak. A night watchman makes his final rounds, singing a traditional watchman's song. As the sun rises on the market place at the foot of the castle, the people of Meeresland sing their opening chorus. Dannoso appears with his three ministers and sings "Ich bin Wer."

Dannoso and the ministers go back into the castle, where the day's orders are given. In the aria, "Ich wünsche mir heute als erstes," Dannoso orders first his dinner, second, pearls and sapphires from the island of Katherina, and third, the abduction of Elena, who is to be brought to Meeresland to become his wife. The Admiral of Meeresland and his men are ordered to carry out the robbery of the pearls and sapphires and the abduction of Elena.

SCENE TWO: The Eisenhut, a commercial vessel under the command of Captain Franz, docks in the Meeresland harbor. Its wares are unloaded, and Franz enjoys a glass of wine with the customs officer. The Admiral and his men, noting that the Eisenhut is well-suited for their mission to Katherina, attempt to commandeer it. Franz and his ship escape at the last moment.

ACT TWO

SCENE ONE: The island of Katherina at twilight. The fishermen return with the day's catch, it is unloaded, and the islanders gather for a collective meal. They sing in their local language a traditional song of thanks, "Laupinini ma Laupanana." A young boy then sings of the simple yet idyllic life of the island: "Meer und Sonne, Wind und Wellen." The people go into their huts for the night, and the boy says goodnight to Elena, who walks pensively to the water's edge.

There she is joined by her mother, who asks her why she has recently seemed distracted. Elena reveals that she is in love with Nemo and wonders if she will ever see him again. After her mother says goodnight, Elena pours out her feelings in the aria "Mein Herz ist voller Bang.'" During the aria she hears a distant voice. It is the oracle of Katherina, who approaches Elena as a sea-gull and is transformed into a young girl when Elena speaks with her. The oracle encourages Elena to be patient and brave and tells her that after a very difficult event, she will be united with Nemo. Duet: "Elena, fasse Mut."

SCENE TWO: Dannoso's men, under the command of the Admiral, land on Katherina. They search the huts to find Elena, drag her out of her little house, and when her mother protests, take her captive, too. Pearls and sapphires are torn from the doors and roofs of the huts and loaded into sacks. Elena, her mother and the booty are taken to the ship, which departs for Meeresland.

ACT THREE

SCENE ONE: Evening in Vulkania. Nemo and his crew arrive back in the grotto and are greeted by the chorus, "Nemo! Nemo!" After inspecting equipment and talking to his men, Nemo sings about his concern for the environment in the aria, "Der blaue Planet, dritter von der Sonne entfernt." He goes to his quarters, remembers Elena and passionately sings the aria, "Elena, Du bist wie die erwärmende Sonne." Overcome by conflict between duty and love, he goes to the pipe organ in his quarters and plays with great agitation.

SCENE TWO: Franz arrives in the grotto and brings news of the planned abduction of Elena by Dannoso. He implores Nemo to assist in rescuing her, but Nemo refuses to help. He and Franz discuss a game of chess, abandoned years before when Franz left Vulkania and went back to the world above. Both have carried with them since that time the placement of the figures on the chessboard. They decide to continue the match, the chess figures are set in place, and Franz and Nemo play the game to its conclusion. The checkmate of the black king by the white queen becomes symbolic for the freeing of Elena. Nemo realizes he must return with Franz to the world above to rescue her, forsaking his undersea life for the love of a beautiful woman.

ACT FOUR

SCENE ONE: Meeresland, early evening. Elena, her mother, and the stolen pearls and sapphires are brought to Dannoso, who tells Elena that she is destined to be his wife. She refuses to marry him and is thrown into prison with her mother. Preparations are made for the 20th anniversary celebration of Dannoso's rule, which will begin after sundown. Alanya appears and performs her belly dance. There are fireworks, and the festival closes raucously. The figures of Nemo and Franz can be seen in the distance, standing on the conning tower of the Nautilus.

SCENE TWO: In the early morning hours, Elena and her mother are unable to sleep. Duet: "Spät in der Nacht." Nemo and Franz quietly free them from their prison cells, while their men make a surprise attack on Meeresland. Nemo and Dannoso fight with swords and Dannoso is mortally wounded. Meeresland, Elena, and her mother are free. Duet: „So ein Segen, so ein Glück." Final chorus: „Die Liebe siegt."

Like that of *Shadow*, *Nemo*'s libretto is mostly set syllabically in simple rhythmic structures with frequently sparse orchestral textures. Van de Vate's rare occasions for ensemble singing allow each individual to project easily, without the added difficulty of a vocal line simultaneously delivering a different text. In some instances, the composer calls for extended vocal techniques such as *Sprechstimme* for text communication. Examining the score's first page (see Example 43), we can see that *Nemo*, like *Shadow*, is conventionally notated and opens with a 32-bar prologue rather than an overture.

Example 43. *Nemo: Jenseits von Vulkania*, mm. 1-9.

PROLOGUE

After the initial timpani roll, the orchestra creeps in layer by layer at tempo ♪=44, with pedal tones entering one and two measures apart in the low strings and brass. Seven measures later, the middle range strings introduce an ostinato, which lasts for the next 22 measures, ending four bars before the prologue's finish. Their simultaneous figures of three, four, and six notes to a beat create a complex rhythmic interplay and lend a dream-like quality to this fantasy opera. Nineteen measures into the prologue, the celesta, marimba, and glockenspiel intensify the dramatic momentum by contributing their own ostinati to the mounting excitement (see Example 44).

Timbral possibilities abound, as Van de Vate incorporates a plethora of percussion instruments as well as celesta, piano, and harp, with divisi winds and brasses. The low, incessant rumble, heard at first primarily in the strings, serves as a backdrop to the gradual introduction of additional orchestra members (like cast members in a play), with flourishes, fanfares, and ostinati suggesting the bubbling of the ocean. This pyramid of tension culminates in the surfacing of the Nautilus with Nemo silhouetted atop, as the full orchestra reaches a loud climax at the original tempo, *langsam* ♪=44, only to fade back to molto lento, *senza battuta* in the prologue's final bar.

Example 44. *Nemo: Jenseits von Vulkania*, mm. 19-21.

Act I begins immediately after the prologue with the "Nachtwächterlied," or the night watchman's song in C Major, softly doubled several octaves higher by piano and piccolo in the key of D-flat Major. The composer refers to this harmonic interplay as "bitonal graffiti." It is already apparent in the opening 18-bar melody that Van de Vate's musical vocabulary in this work consists predominantly of diatonic melodies with less conservative underlying harmonies. The lyrical vocal lines are what she refers to as "twentieth-century tonal," set in simple rhythms and offering little opportunity for melismatic vocal displays. The singers stay challenged, however, as their parts teem with changing meters.

Although the orchestra is clearly secondary in importance to the vocalists, it always serves to enhance and promote characterization and drama. Its secondary role is relinquished only during sporadic "non-vocal" interludes, where the normally sparse texture is replaced by a densely layered full ensemble. As in *Shadow*, *Nemo* calls for little ensemble singing, and most of those sections are sung in dialogue. There are, however, several choral interludes in the opera. A large mixed chorus and the men's chorus appear three times in the first act, singing mostly in triadic harmony. The first mixed chorus, which follows the "Nachtwächterlied," is set in four, sometimes five highly syncopated parts, almost entirely in parallel "block" chords (see Example 45).

Example 45. *Nemo: Jenseits von Vulkania*, mm. 185-189.

The mixed chorus returns briefly later in the act, singing together with the children's chorus for just four bars. Then shortly after, the men's chorus, representing a band of sailors, sings a lively four-part offstage chorus in tribute to their captain. At the opening of Act II, the mixed chorus sings an authentic Polynesian hymn as a celebration of the day's catch and their evening feast. Van de Vate adds a sacred touch to this folk hymn by scoring it antiphonally for boy soprano and choir. Choruses appear again on two occasions: the four-part men's chorus sings at the beginning of Act III, and the mixed chorus closes the piece at the end of Act IV during an elaborate display of fireworks.

Throughout the opera, the composer maintains a lyric style, sometimes writing in popular or folk idioms, with simple, frequently minor mode melodies. Indications of the popular idiom abound. In the middle of Act I, Van de Vate requests that the clarinets play "mit Blues-Qualität" (with blues quality), and uses percussion instruments reminiscent of the New Orleans blues style, namely hi-hat cymbal and snare drum played with brushes. The syncopated compound meter groove is answered by a "senza vibrato, bluesy" oboe (see Example 46). A more exotic folk touch is added with the Polynesian hymn, and instruments such as cabasa, temple blocks, and marimba, as well as the Polynesian language, help contribute to the island flavor.

Example 46, *Nemo: Jenseits von Vulkania*, mm 699-705

Musical and Dramatic Flow

Three representative arias from *Nemo* are discussed in order to convey a sense of the opera's musical and dramatic narrative: Dannoso's back-to-back arias, "Ich bin Wer" and "Ich wünsche mir heute als erstes," and Nemo's "Elena, Du bist wie die erwärmende Sonne."

As the evil dictator Dannoso appears with his three ministers at the beginning of Act I, he sings "Ich bin Wer," a highly disjunct aria filled with heavy, detached articulations and syncopations. Singing of his own greatness, the egomaniac is at first accompanied primarily by bass instruments, which drive the tempo by heavily pulsing each beat. Low strings, bassoon, and horns answer the timpani's downbeat attacks with staccato on beats two and three. During the first orchestral interlude (four pages into the aria), the higher winds scream a "schrill lärmendes gliss." (shrill, raucous glissando) as if in warning to anyone who might dare defy the powerful villain (see Example 47).

Example 47. *Nemo: Jenseits von Vulkania*, mm. 249-252.

As the aria progresses, energy is intensified. The orchestral texture thickens, and the percussion section increases its forces. Abrupt octave leaps in both the vocal and orchestral parts, set sporadically throughout the clamorous musical fabric, create a diabolical stinging effect. Then after a 23-bar orchestral interlude, Dannoso's ministers inquire about his orders for the day.

18 bars later, Dannoso hurls himself into a second aria, giving his orders for the day. Since the three ministers ask him in turn what his wishes are, he responds in three parts. First he describes the elaborate menu upon which he expects to feast in half an hour, complete with albatross, buttered beets, crunchy bacon, a very dark, rich sauce, and flavorful, strong wine. The orchestral accompaniment for this aria is lighter than in the previous one, but has a similarly strong rhythmic drive. In this "gastronomic" section, the figure ♫♪, set in consecutive tritones, mirrors the tritones in Dannoso's vocal part. The rhythm is first passed from clarinet to English horn, then later from bassoon back to clarinet (see Example 48). The percussion punctuates each menu choice with brief interpolations between descriptions of food items.

Dannoso's next demand is for precious gems, sapphires, and pearls from the island of Katherina. During much of this section, unyielding motor rhythms, ♫♫, from the treble instruments, and ♪♪♪ from the bass instruments propel the aria forward until Dannoso arrives at his third and final command: the kidnapping of Elena.

Example 48. *Nemo: Jenseits von Vulkania,* mm. 392-403.

The earlier ♪♪♪ rhythmic motive returns, combined with the motoric rhythms of the second section, ♪♪♪♪ and ♪♪♪. After several tempo shifts reflecting his erratic behavior, an irate Dannoso orders his ministers to get out, screaming, "Bringt mir! Bringt mir! Bringt mir..." Nine bars of triplets ensue, maintaining the omnipresent, almost evil rhythmic drive. Finally, the orchestra fades, leaving Dannoso with a lone timpani roll. He exclaims in *Sprechstimme*, "das werd' ich alles besitzen! Ha ha ha ha..." (I will have it all!)

Nemo's second aria, "Elena, Du bist wie die erwärmende Sonne" (Elena, you are like the warming sun) occurs in Act III. After a melancholy oboe prelude of six measures, Nemo begins to sing his beloved's name, "Elena," doubled by marimba. As he continues, three solo violins and solo viola play interweaving countermelodies. Nemo's beautiful, plaintive A minor love song is set primarily in conjunct motion, with an abundance of smooth, wave-like triplets. The warmth of Nemo's love for Elena is reflected in Van de Vate's orchestration with its focus on harp, vibraphone, English horn, and oboe. She reserves the brass and bass instruments for the occasional tuneful interjection or drone-like chord. Throughout the aria, the orchestral texture remains rather sparse, with instruments making their entrances and exits unobtrusively. Unhurried waves of sound in a relaxed tempo (ranging from ♪=44 to ♪=66) seem to suspend time as Nemo pours out his lovesick reverie. He sings of the earth's light, which he misses deep in the ocean, and laments that he cannot bring Elena to his world, that "the sun will not caress her face, and her eyes cannot reflect a starry night." At his mention of sunshine, piano and celesta enter with a unison slow trill for six beats, as if representing a sunrise, and continue for one measure with an echo of Nemo's vocal line (see Example 49).

Example 49. *Nemo: Jenseits von Vulkania*, mm. 226-229.

Nemo struggles mightily with his feelings, torn between his love for Elena and his commitment to continuing his father's work. At the end, the music reaches a climax as he cries out "Elena! Elena!" In a particularly melodramatic gesture, he then crashes over to his pipe organ and plays the toccata from Bach's *Toccata and Fugue in D Minor* as the curtain falls on the third act.

Performance Considerations

The singers' parts lie comfortably within their vocal ranges and the orchestration is supportive rather than antagonistic. However, the vocal parts are sometimes very exposed and require confident execution of numerous tempo and meter changes. In typical Van de Vate style, the dramatic forces – lead character, boy soprano, men's chorus, belly dancer and fireworks – all combine in perfect syntax, with a fluid elision of scenes and events. Obviously, ample rehearsal time is a necessity for both vocalists and instrumentalists. The percussionists especially have a myriad of instruments with which to contend.

The technical requirements for mounting a production of Nemo are perhaps even greater than the musical ones. Thus, a full technical staff is a prerequisite, including artistic director, conductor, stage manager, set designer, lighting designer, costume/make-up designer, and properties manager. The set must not only have a 1900s South Seas flavor, but also accommodate a large cast; it must also frame bulky set pieces such as Franz's ship, Nemo's pipe organ, and Dannoso's throne. In two of the four sets, two different scenes occur, one indoors and one outdoors. For example, Act I, Scene 1 begins outside in the Meeresland marketplace, where Dannoso sings his first aria, then moves inside the castle for his second aria. Similarly, Nemo starts Act III on the submarine deck in the undersea grotto of Vulkania and ends in his quarters, passionately crooning over his beloved Elena. Since the time allowed for orchestrally accompanied set changes is minimal, sets should be built for optimum mobility.

In some cases, properties seem large enough to be considered part of the set. The chess pieces in Act III, for instance, should be discernible from the audience, and both the ship and the chessmen need to be maneuvered within the set as part of the stage action. In a busy opera such as this one, all components, large and small, must be carefully planned and coordinated.

Lighting is also of particular importance in this opera, since there are scenes at sunrise and twilight, as well as on land and under the sea. Nemo's silhouette atop his submarine during the prologue is relatively easily accomplished, but Act IV's fireworks present another set of challenges. The use of a scrim might be helpful for some of the lighting effects, such as those in the prologue.

Nemo is a creative costume designer's dream with its combination of period costumes and exotic settings. Ranging from the royal finery of the evil Dannoso and the Katherinians' native Polynesian attire to the practical uniforms of Nemo and his crew, the opera provides rich opportunity for elaborate, unusual costumes.

CONCLUSION

In all of Nancy Van de Vate's theatrical vocal works, she taps into many different tonal and atonal idioms. Her earlier theater pieces, *A Night in the Royal Ontario Museum* and *Cocaine Lil*, use a more typically 20th-century idiom, with a wide variety of extended vocal techniques as well as aleatory, chromaticism, extensive use of tritones, motor rhythms, *ostinati, Sprechstimme*, and displaced octaves. In both works, the form is largely through-composed, with only occasional reminders of earlier melodies.

The composer's operas are stylistically more conservative than her shorter vocal works. Though neither opera's form can be categorized as that found in the traditional number operas of the classical era, both works are romantic in nature and construction. They possess an organic quality as individual sections gradually evolve into one another. Their music is highly lyrical and predominantly diatonic, with much more idiomatic and conjunct melodic lines than in either of the shorter works. Both of those overflow with disjunct, chromatic melodies and tend to sound musically more adventurous.

The short duration and small staging requirements of *Night* and *Cocaine Lil* make both pieces quite portable. Though the works present considerable musical challenges, their production demands are minor in comparison to the larger works. As mentioned earlier, each of the operas would require a technical staff for a successful production.

Despite these differences in musical language, Van de Vate's stylistic hallmark, timbral exploration within a lyrical context, remains central to all four works, whether in the electronic sounds and vocal effects of *Night*, the nonsense syllables, layered vocal effects, and percussion in *Cocaine Lil*, or in the painstaking, distinctive orchestration of *Shadow* and *Nemo*. In the two operas in particular, Van de Vate stretches traditional instruments to their limits in order to create otherworldly mixtures of sound. She also upholds her reputation as one of today's most exciting composers for percussion.

With the greatest respect for the text itself, she allows the rhythm of words to dictate the rhythm of the music, setting almost everything syllabically. In turn, she allows the rhythm of the text to shape the melodies, which even in the most disjunct of Cocaine Lil's outcries sound profoundly human.

Van de Vate is a very precise composer, always incorporating many specific tempo, dynamic, and articulation indications, as well as more general commentary about the mood and setting of the works. On the other hand, her music is never dry or overly cerebral; with or without words, it speaks directly to the listener. Her use of musical quotation (the Chopin funeral march in *Cocaine Lil*, the Bach Toccata in D minor in *Nemo*, for example) gives the listener points of entry into a 20th century musical language that might otherwise seem alien. From the performer's perspective, these pieces are not generally showcases for technical virtuosity, but rather for profound musicianship and narrative development.

BIBLIOGRAPHY

Ellis, Stephen. "Nancy Van de Vate," Contemporary Composers. Chicago: St. James Press, 1992.

Ellis, Stephen. "Review of Nancy Van de Vate, Krakow Concerto for percussion and orchestra, Katyn for orchestra and chorus." Fanfare 14 #4 (March/April 1991), p. 411.

Gann, Kyle. "Review of Nancy Van de Vate, Distant Worlds, Dark Nebulae, Journeys, Concertpiece for Cello and Small Orchestra," Fanfare 11, #3 (January/February, 1988), p. 224.

LePage, Jane. Women Composers, Conductors, and Musicians of the 20th Century. Metuchen: Scarecrow Press, 1980.

Loft, Kurt. "Tones of Anguish." The Tampa Tribune. 21 May 1989.

Mackey, Jocelyn. "Review of Nancy Van de Vate, Distant Worlds, Dark Nebulae, Joumeys, Concertpiece for Cello and Small orchestra."Pan Pipes #2 (Winter 1988): p. 15.

Van de Vate, Nancy. Interview by Michelle Vought, 1 August 1993. Tape recording, Vienna, Austria.

DISCOGRAPHY

Nancy Van de Vate: Chamber Music Vol. V. Michelle Vought, soprano. Vienna Modern Masters VMM 2028, 1998.
"A Night in the Royal Ontario Museum"

Nancy Van de Vate: Chamber Music Vol. VI. Michelle Vought, soprano, with accompanying vocal quartet. Vienna Modern Masters VMM 2034, 1998.
"Cocaine Lil"

Nancy Van de Vate: Opera and Music Theater Vol: IV. Blair Resicka, mezzo-soprano, with accompanying vocal quartet. Vienna Modern Masters VMM 2026, 1998.
"Cocaine Lil"

Nancy Van de Vate: Opera and Music Theater Vol. III, Michelle Vought, soprano, Slovak Radio Orchestra. Vienna Modern Masters VMM 4003, 2001.
"In the Shadow of the Glen"

Nancy Van de Vate: Opera and Music Theater II, Michelle Vought, Moravian Philharmonic, Vienna Modern Masters VMM 4002, 2001.
"Nemo: Jenseits von Vulkania"

Nancy Van de Vate: Music from Six Continents, 1992 series, Krakow Radio Symphony Orchestra, Szymon Kawalla,, conductor, VMM 3008, 1992.
"Dark Nebulae"

Michelle Vought

A specialist in contemporary music, Michelle Vought has recorded nine works for Vienna Modern Masters. In 2005 she produced and performed in the world premiere of Nancy Van de Vate's latest opera, *Where the Cross Is Made*. Professor of Voice at Illinois State University, she also maintains an international performing career.